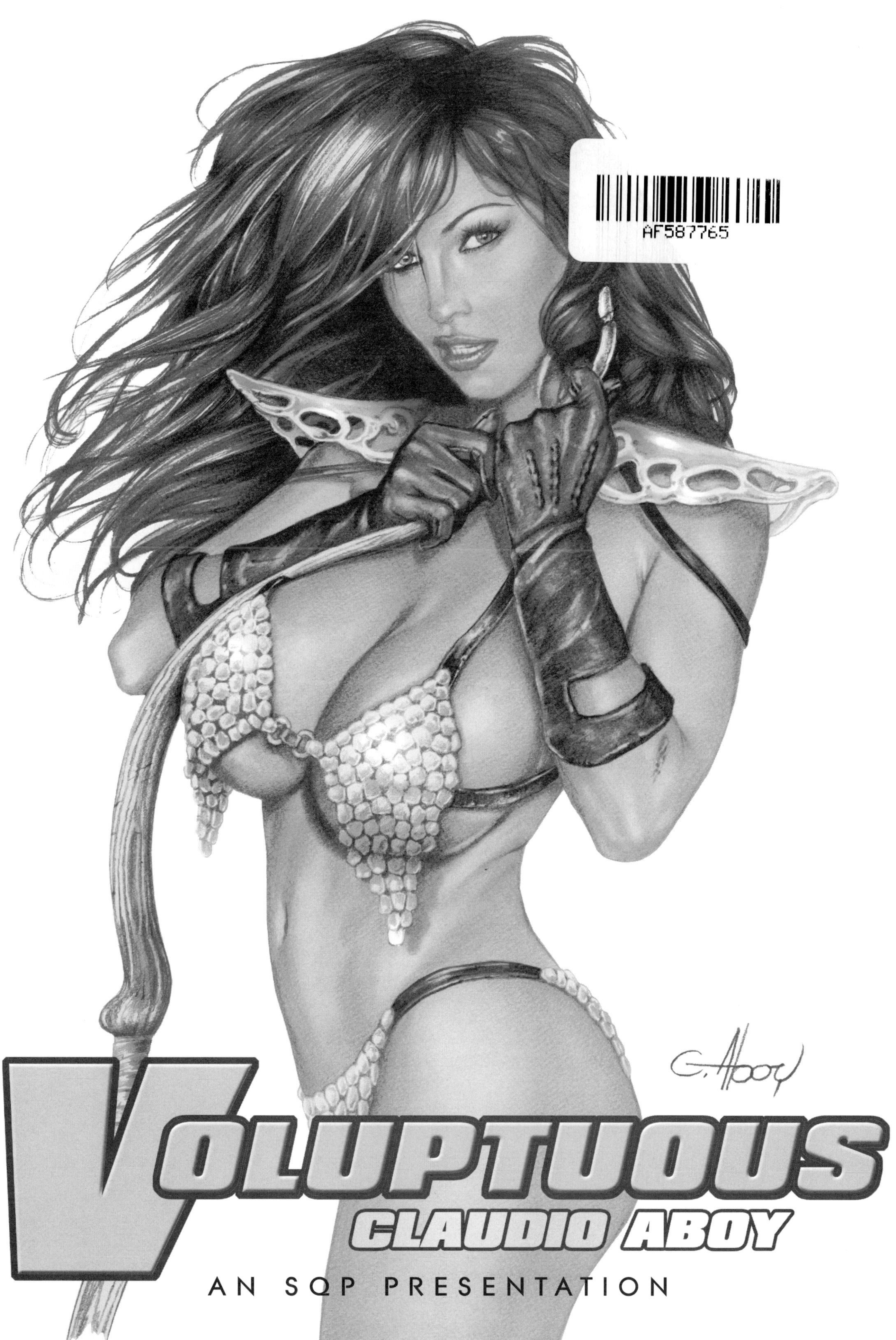

VOLUPTUOUS
CLAUDIO ABOY
AN SQP PRESENTATION

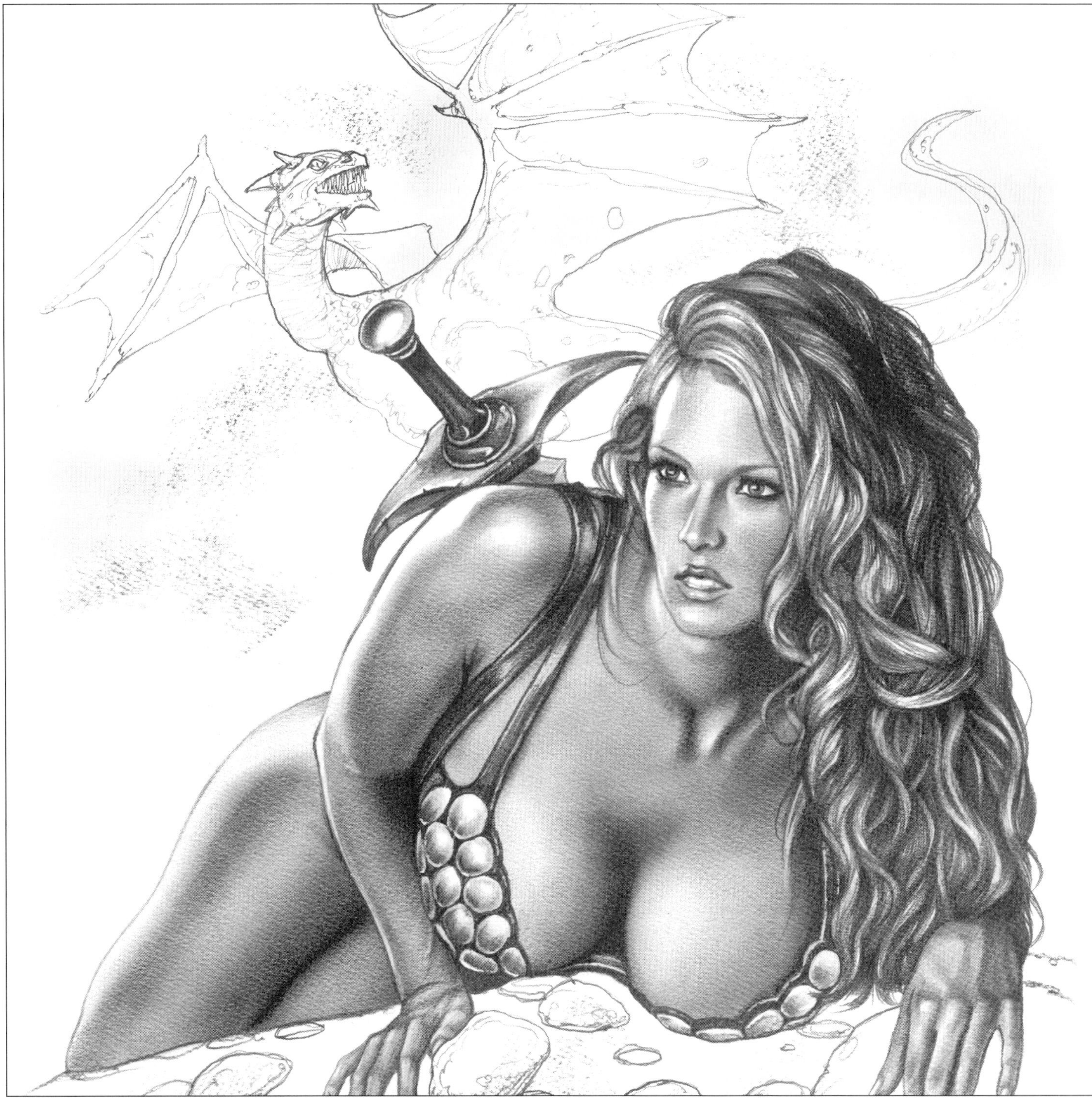

VOLUPTUOUS

Volume One

Book design by Grassy Knoll Studios.

Published by
SQP Inc.
PO Box 248 - Columbus, NJ 08022

Sal Quartuccio & Bob Keenan - Publishers

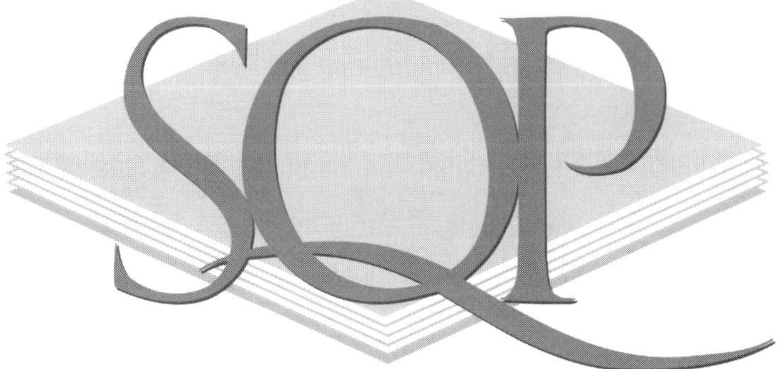

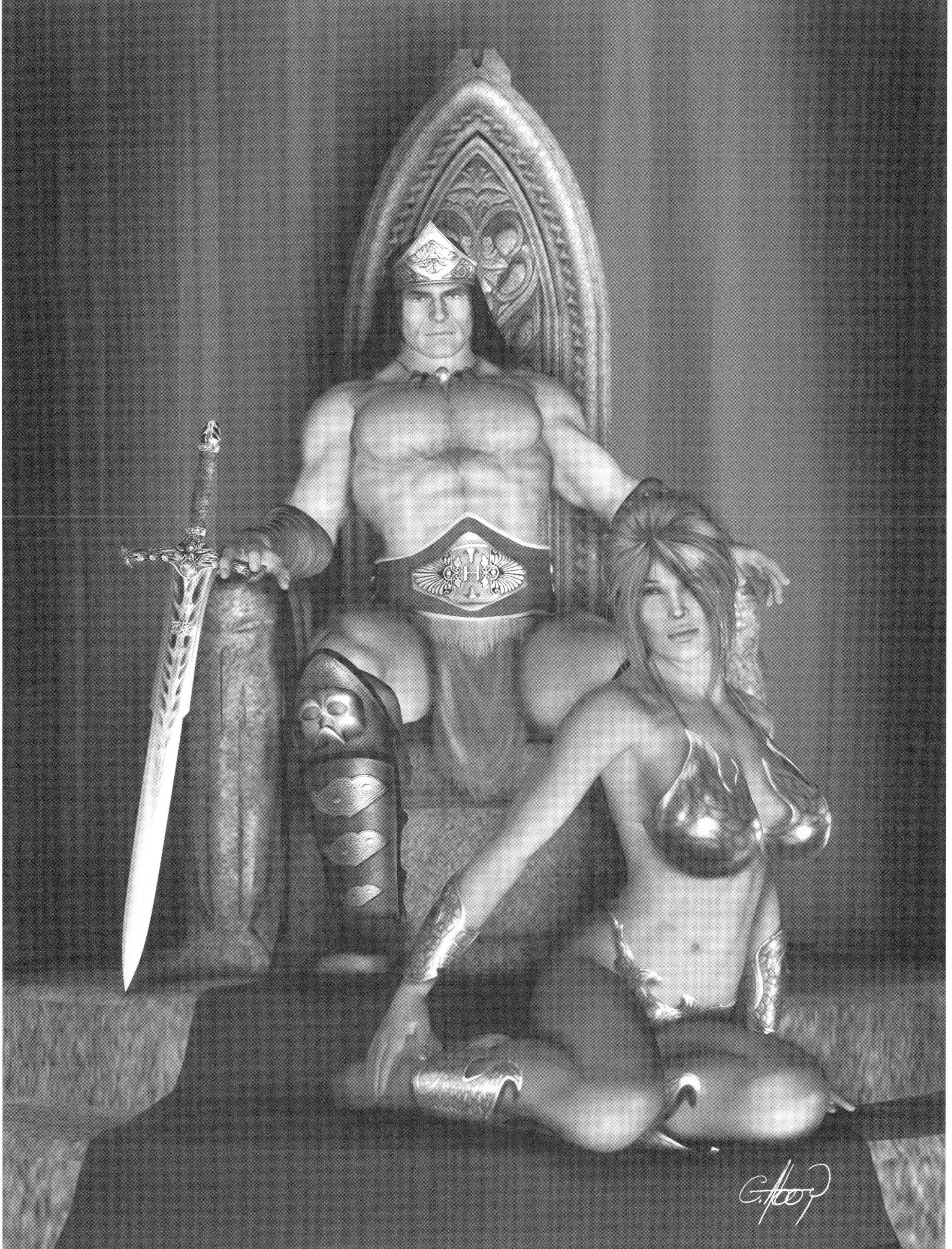

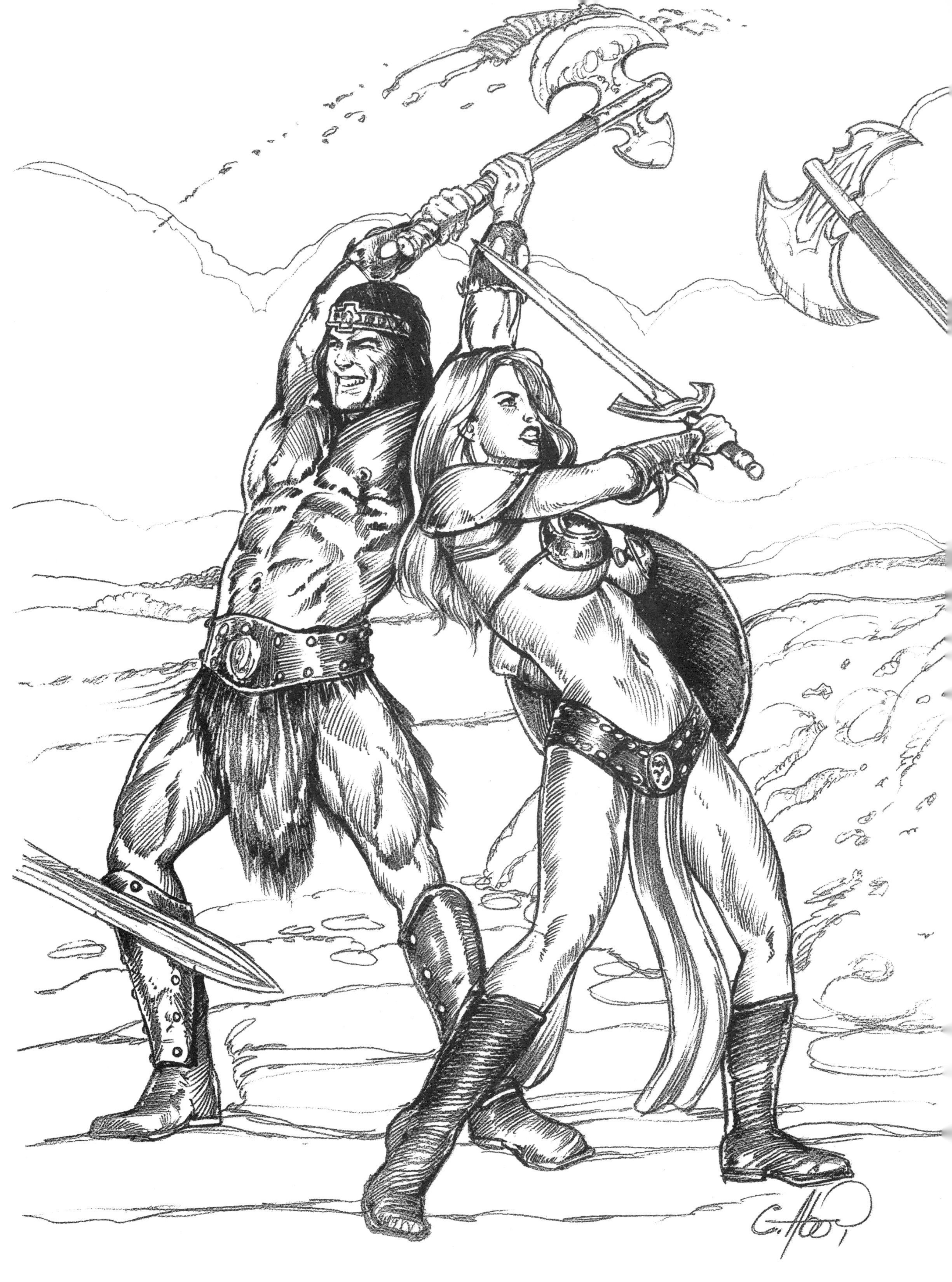

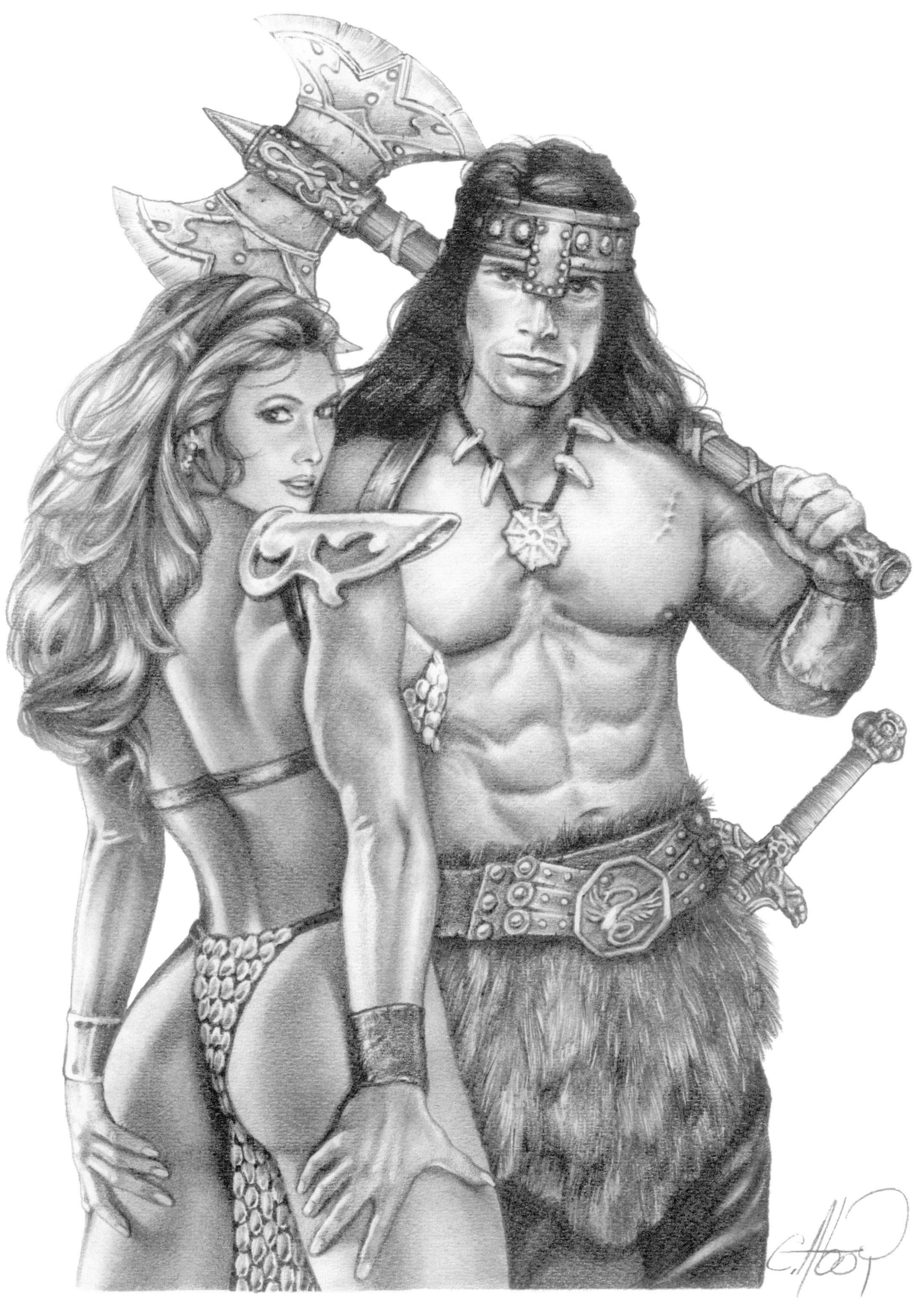

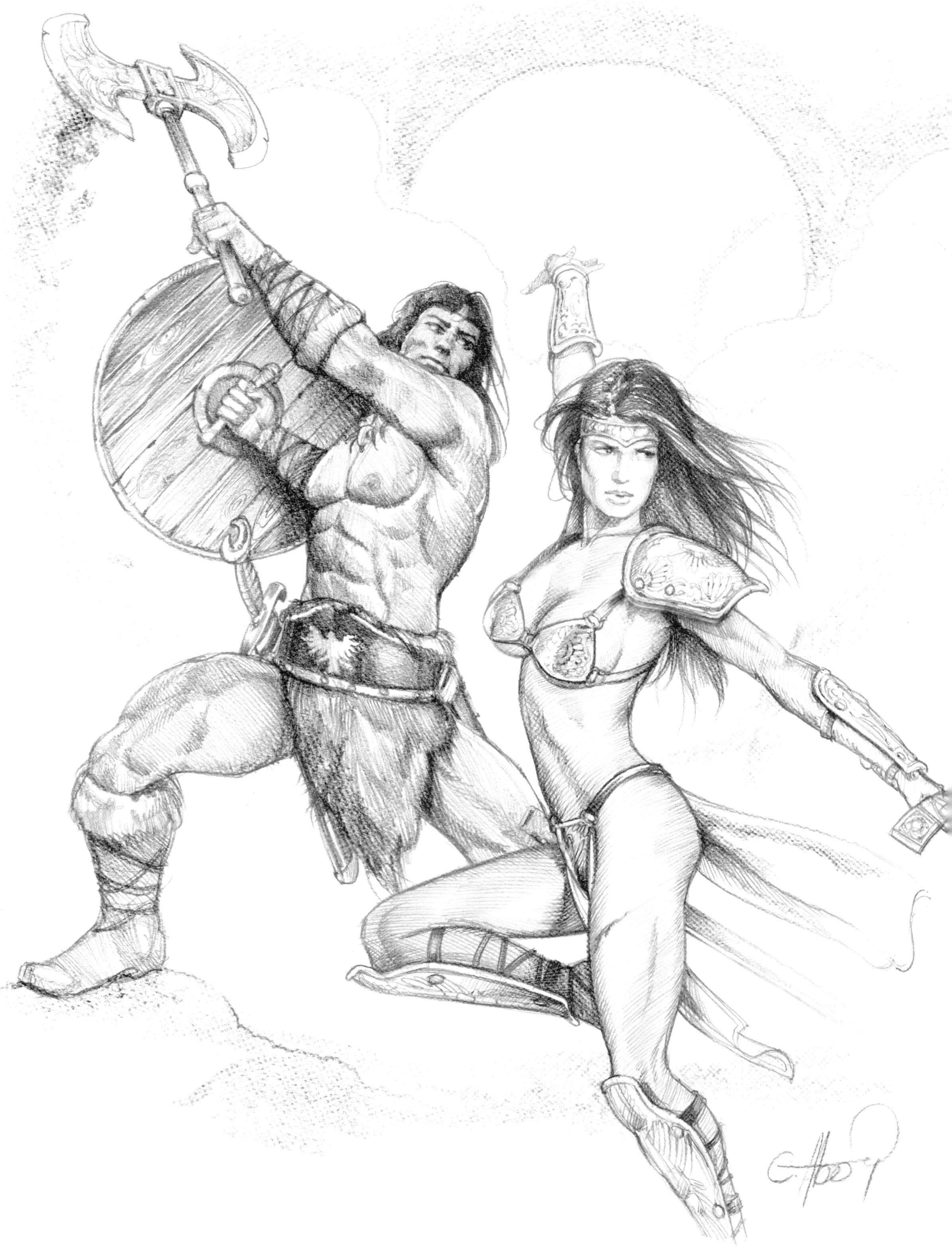

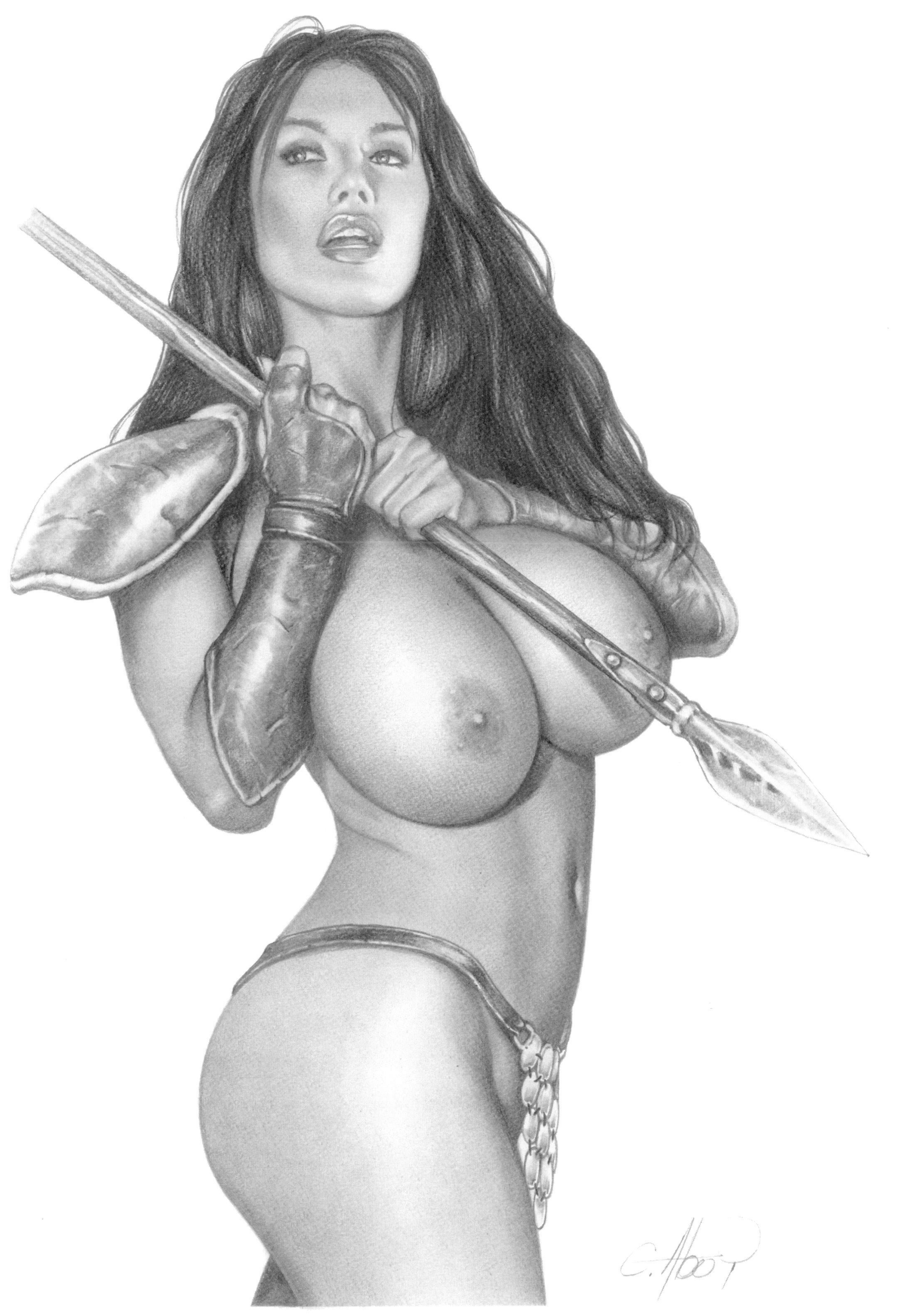

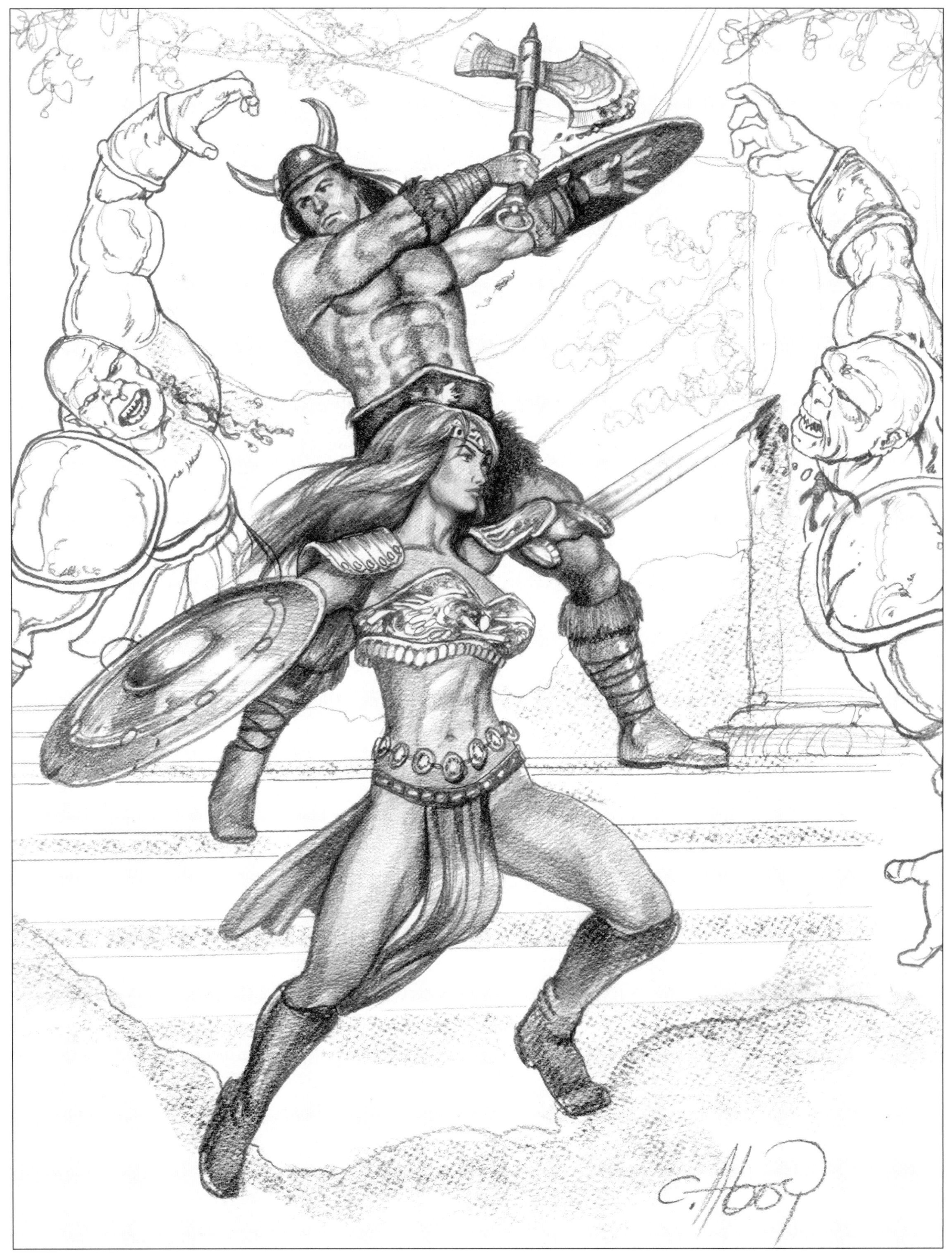

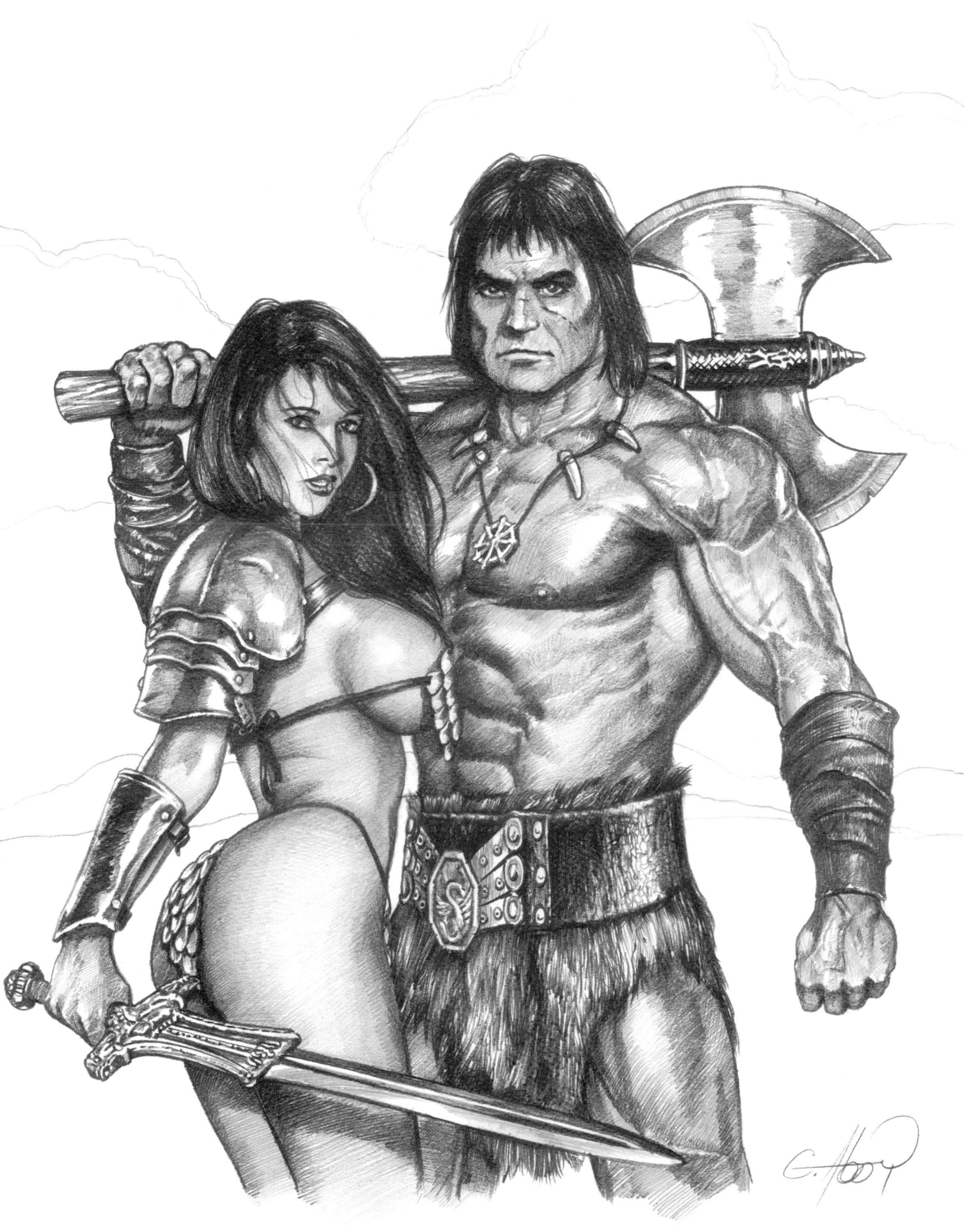

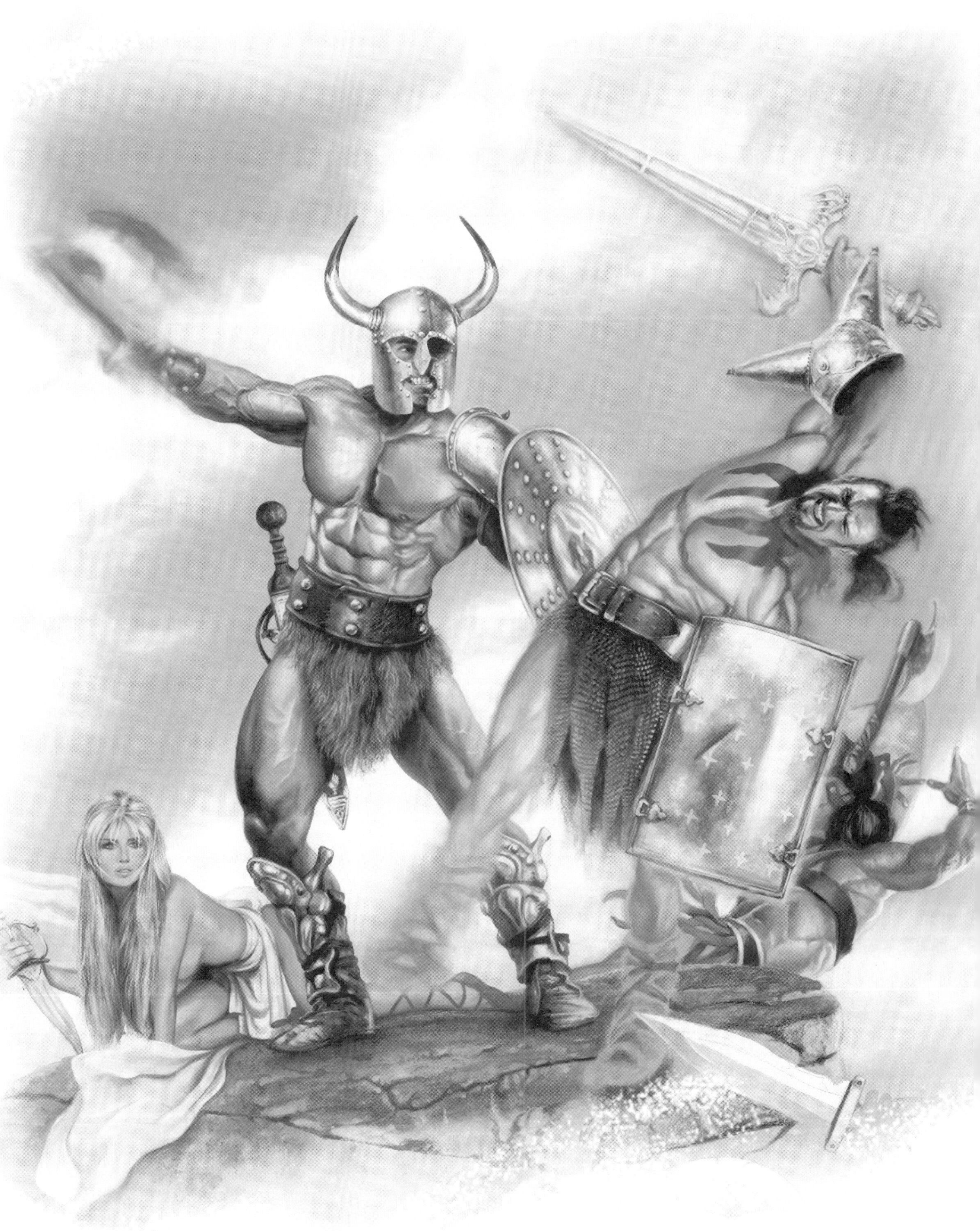

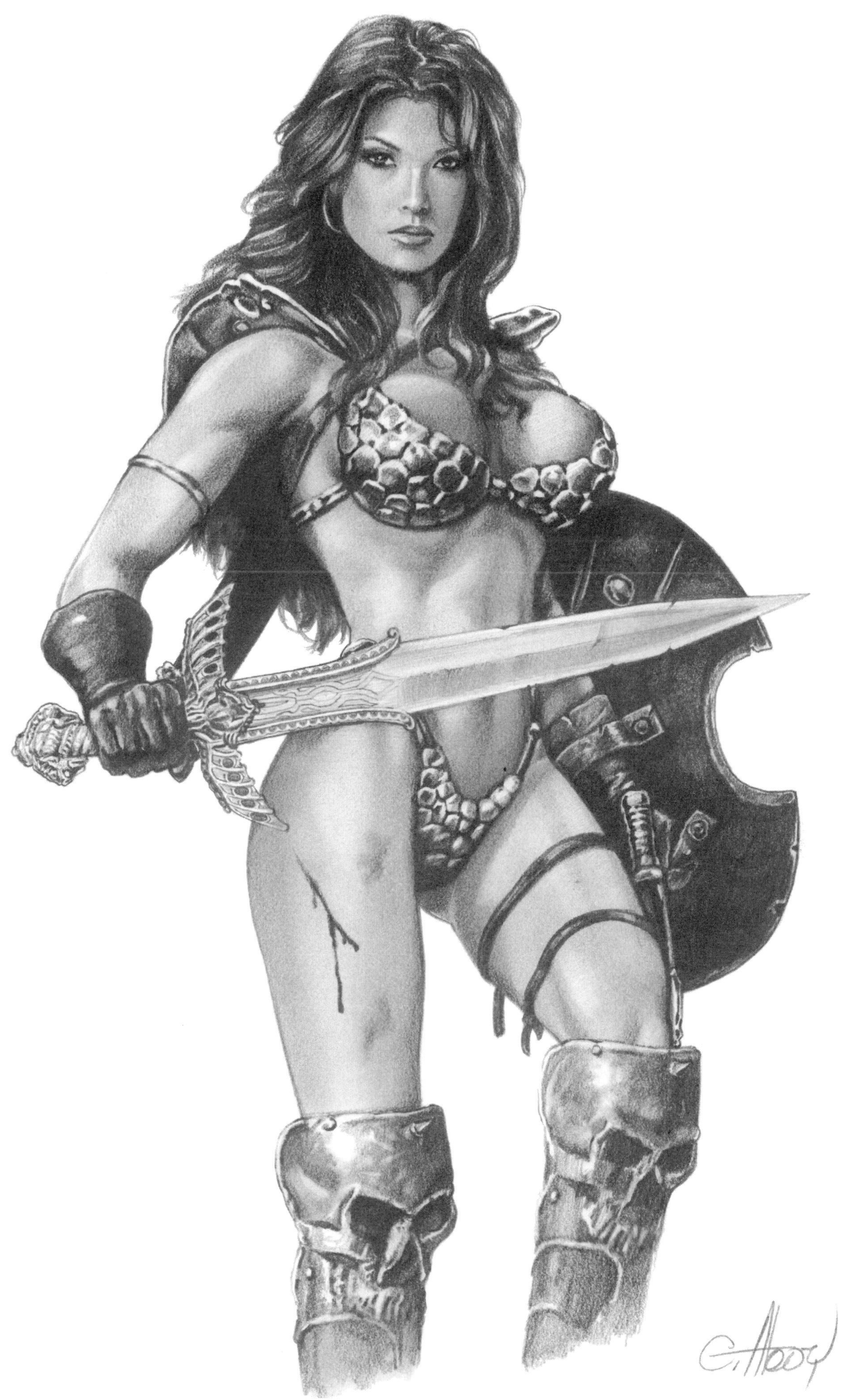

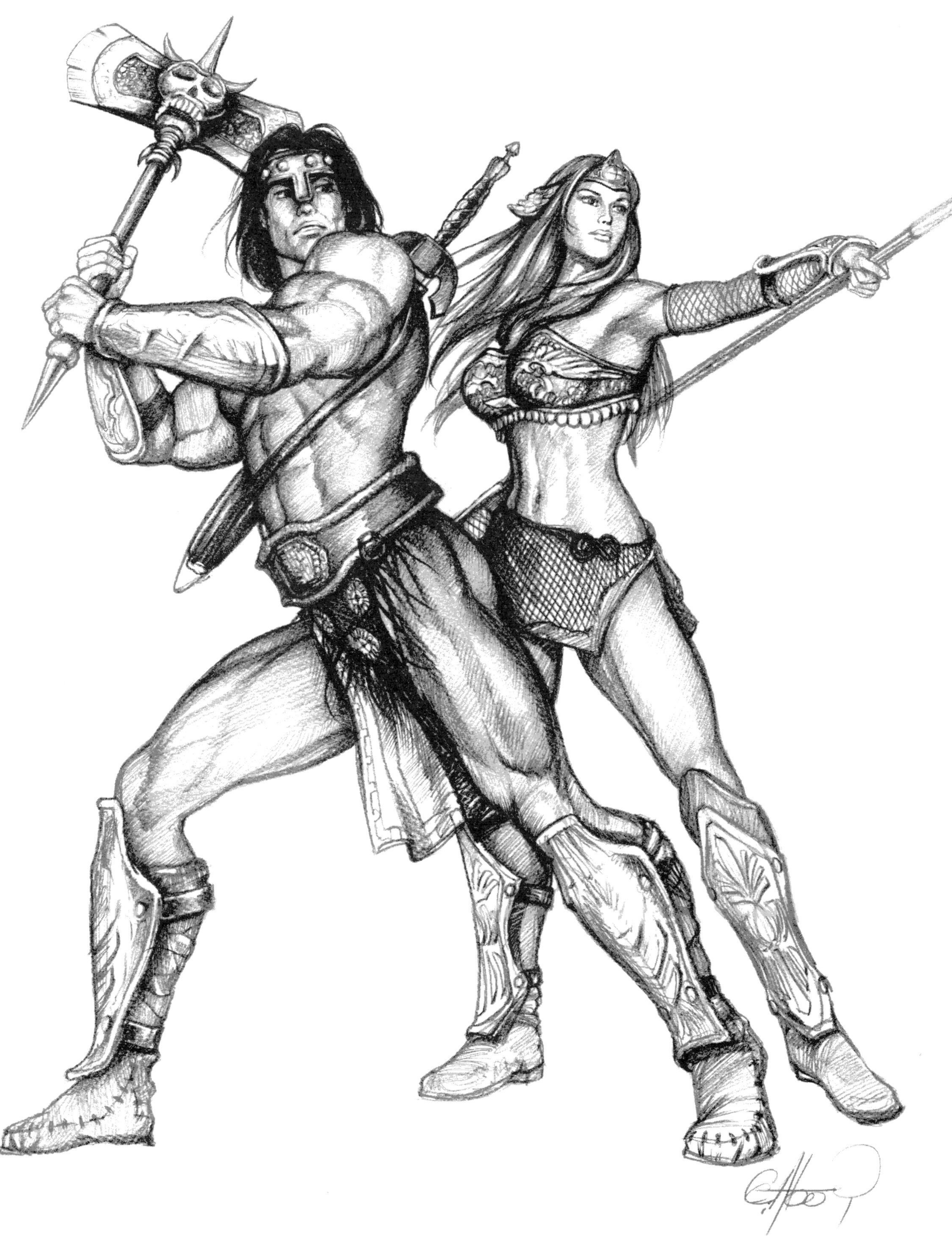

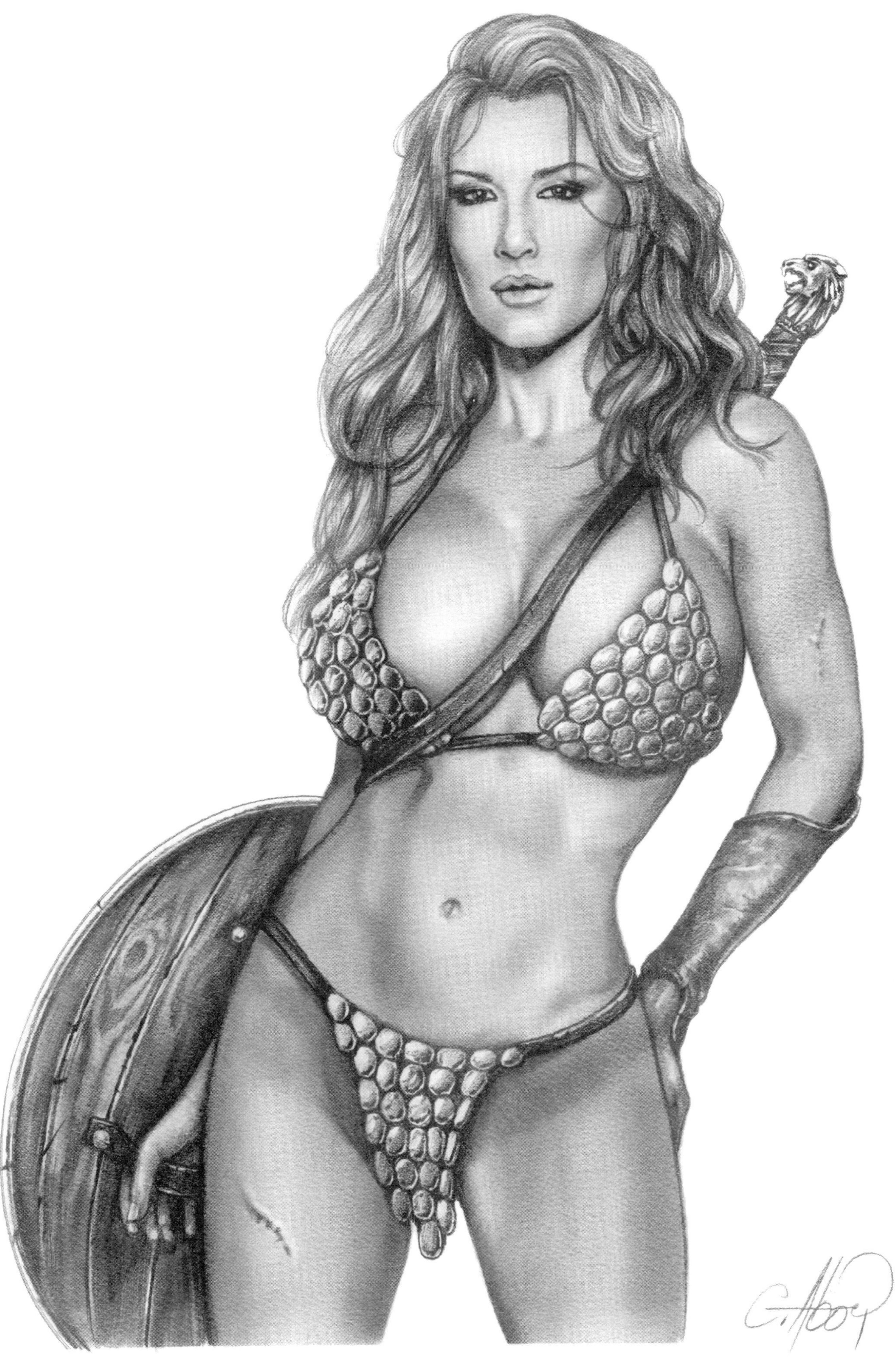

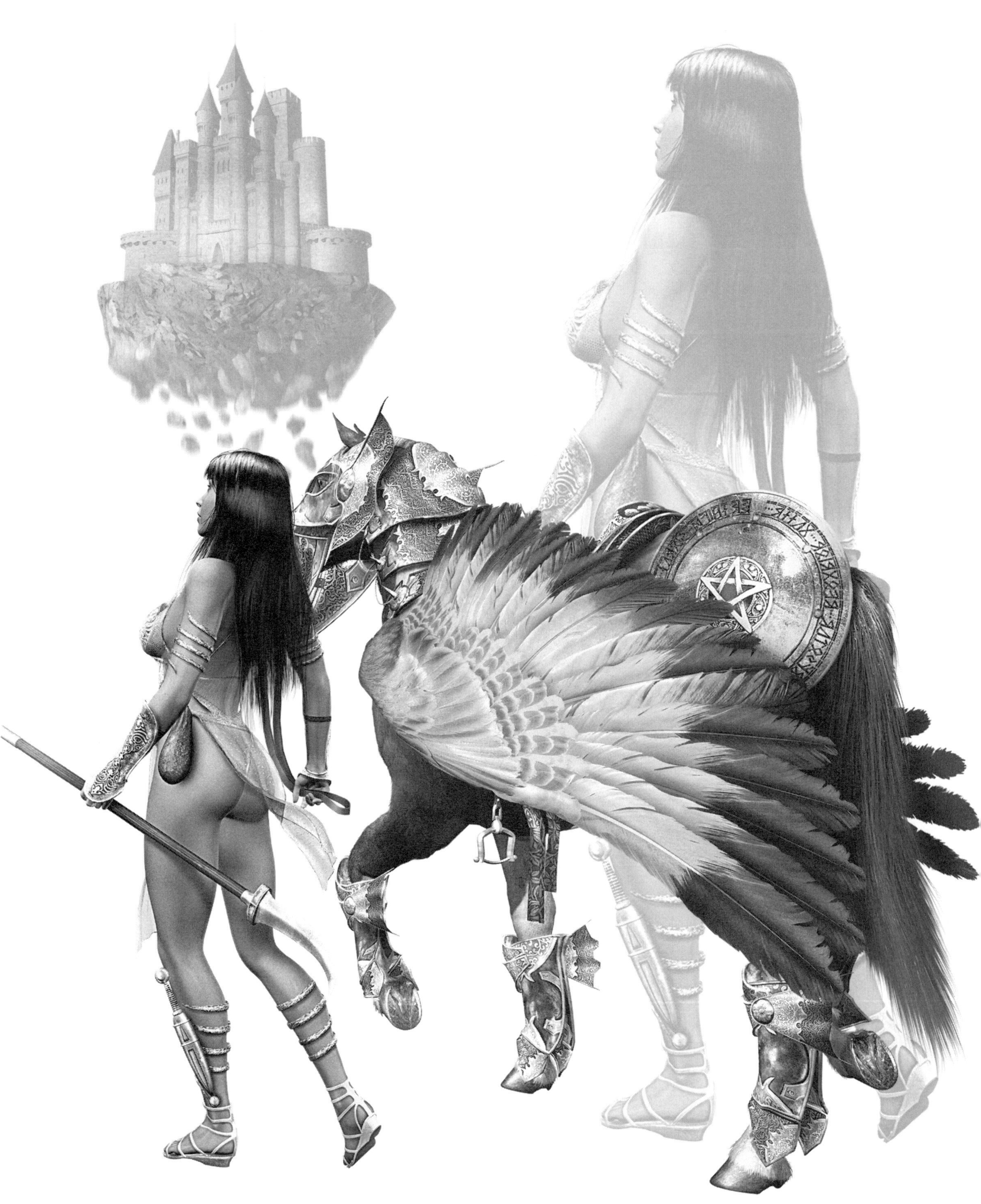

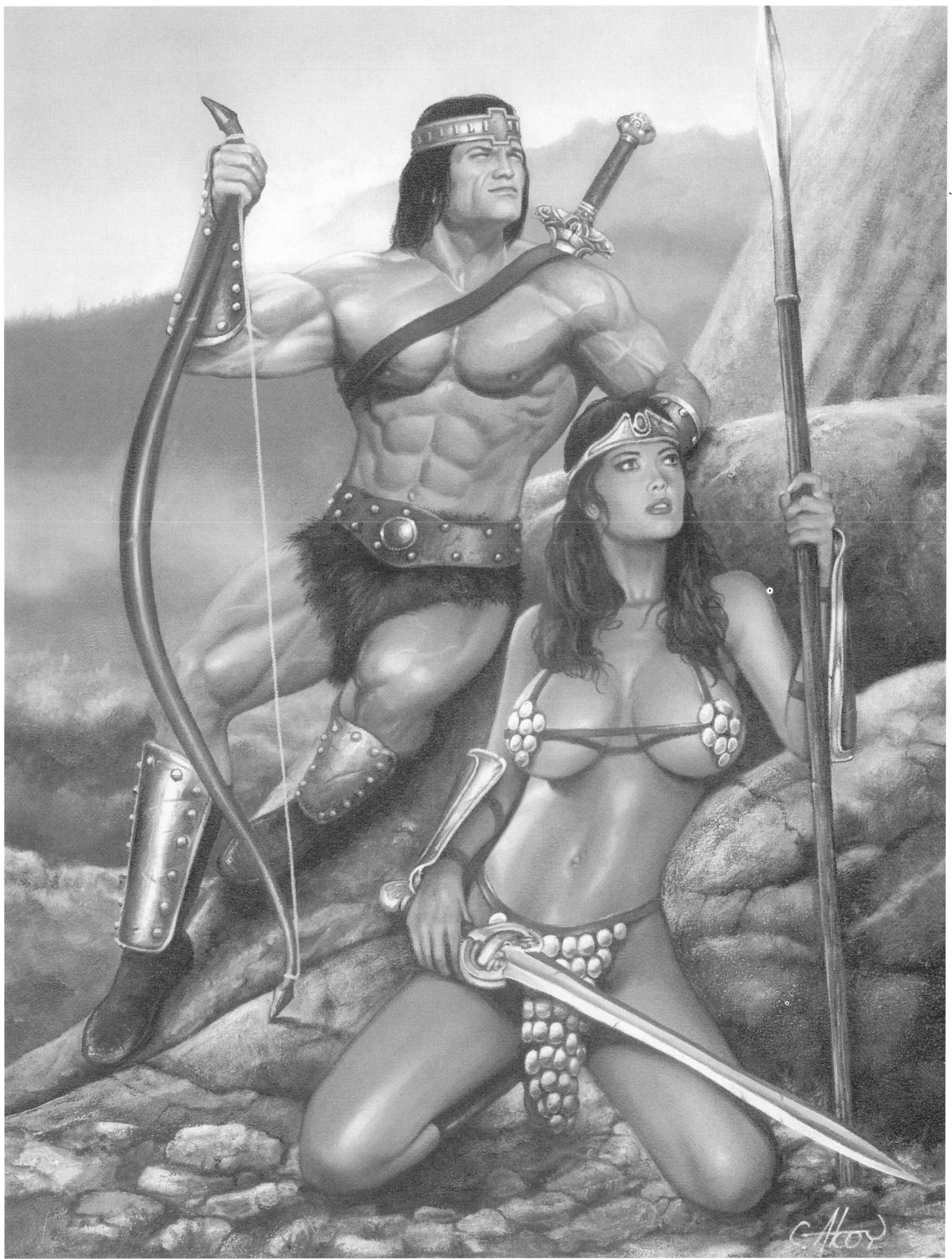
C. Alcoy

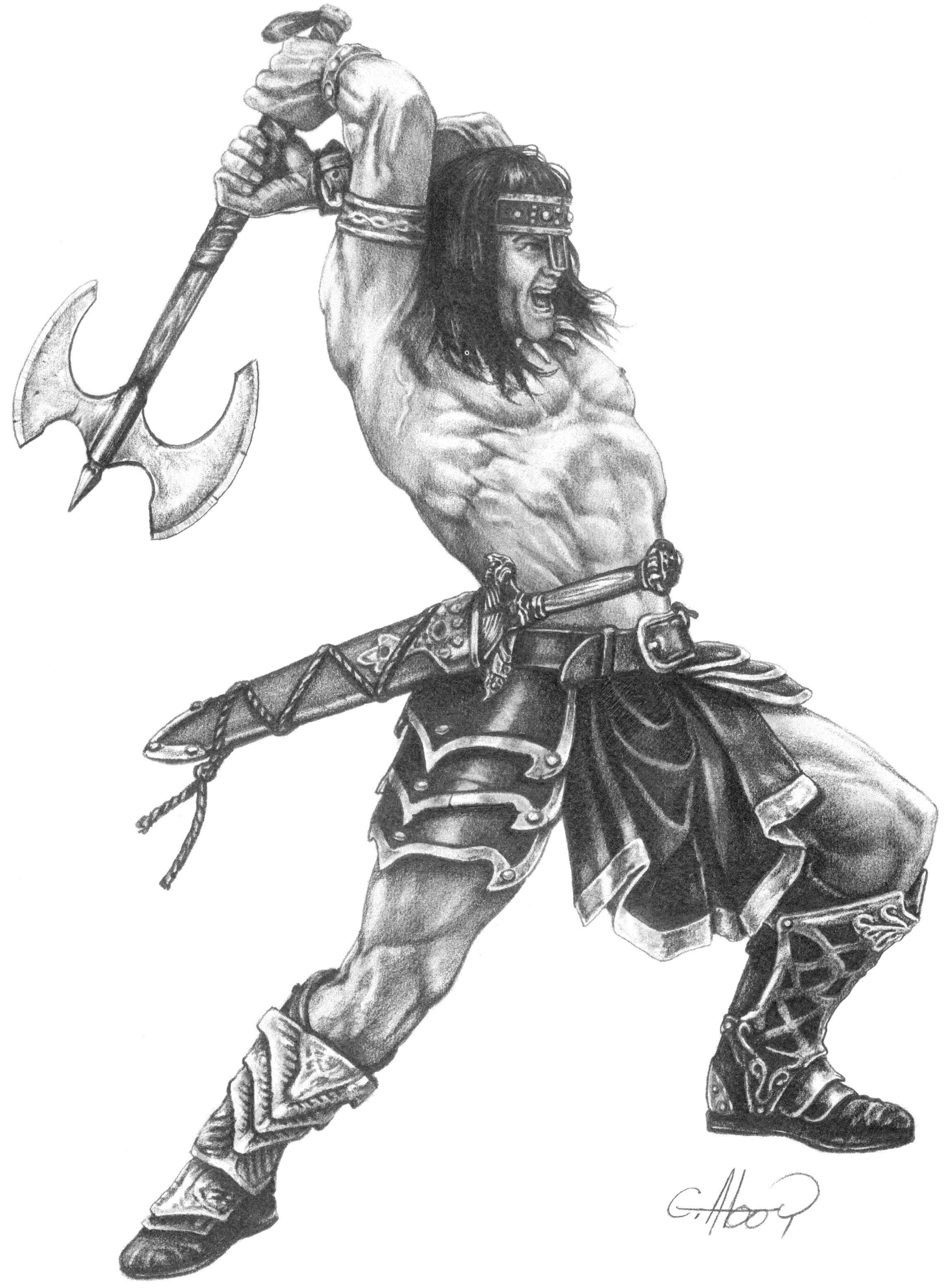

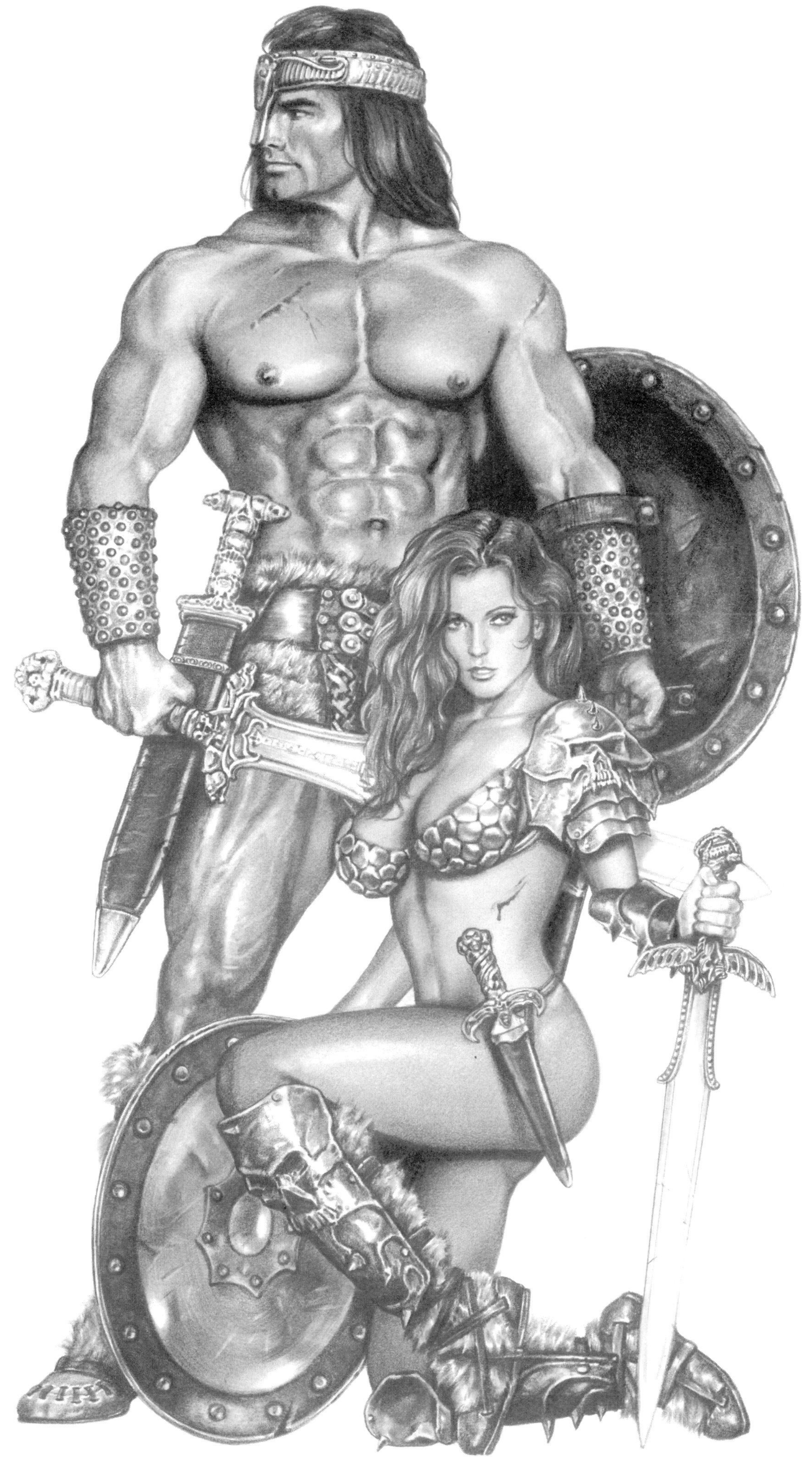

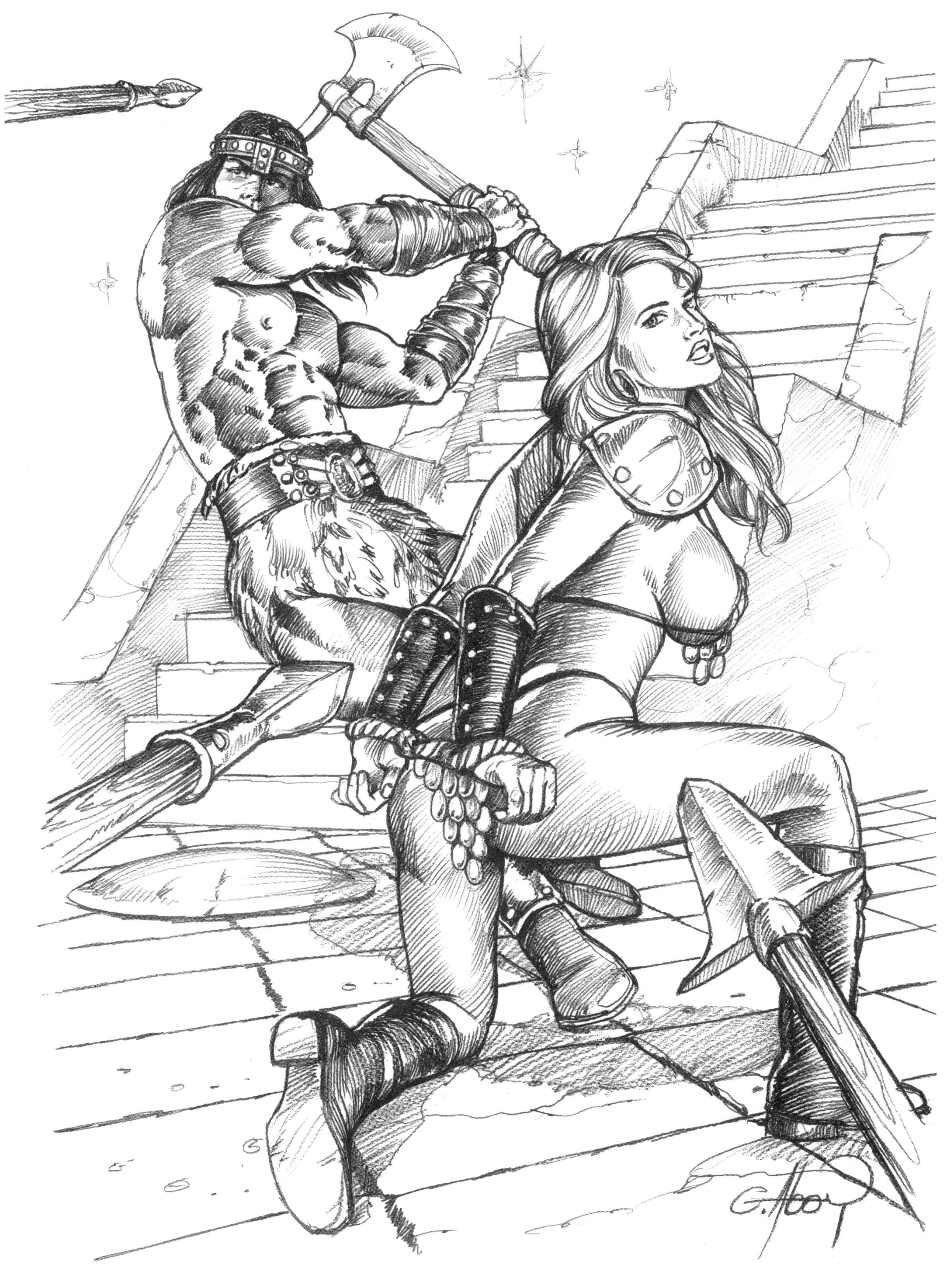

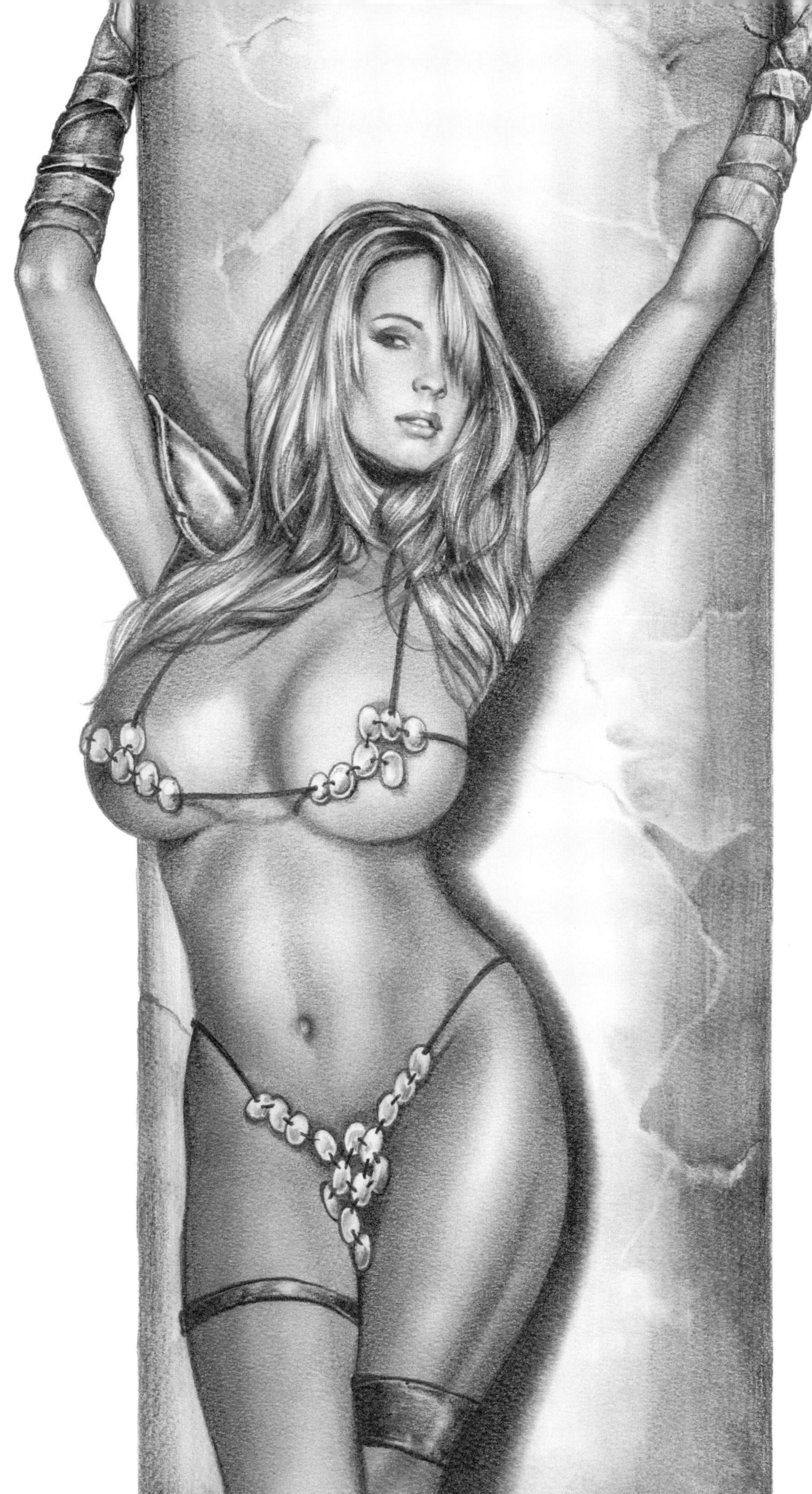

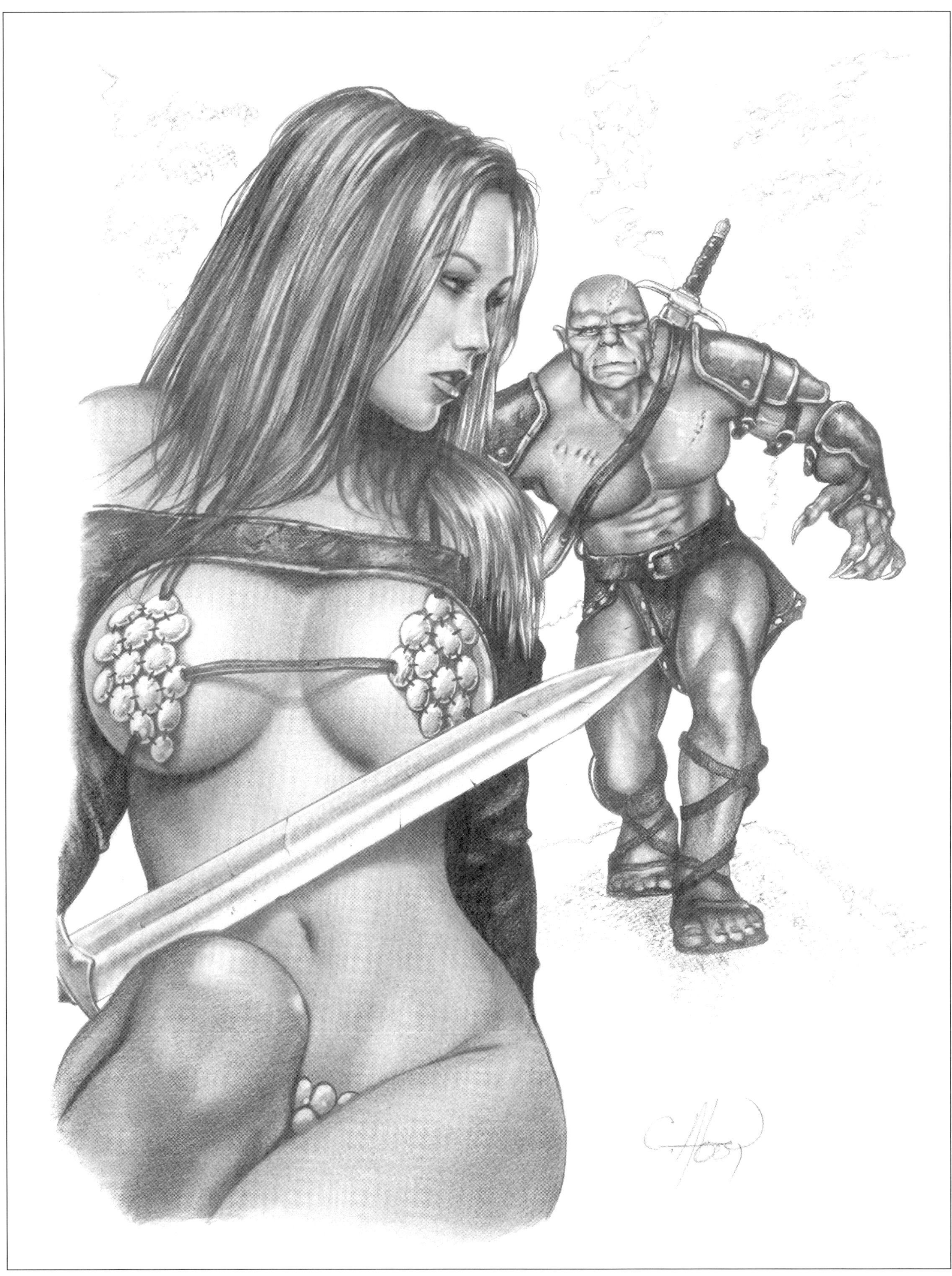

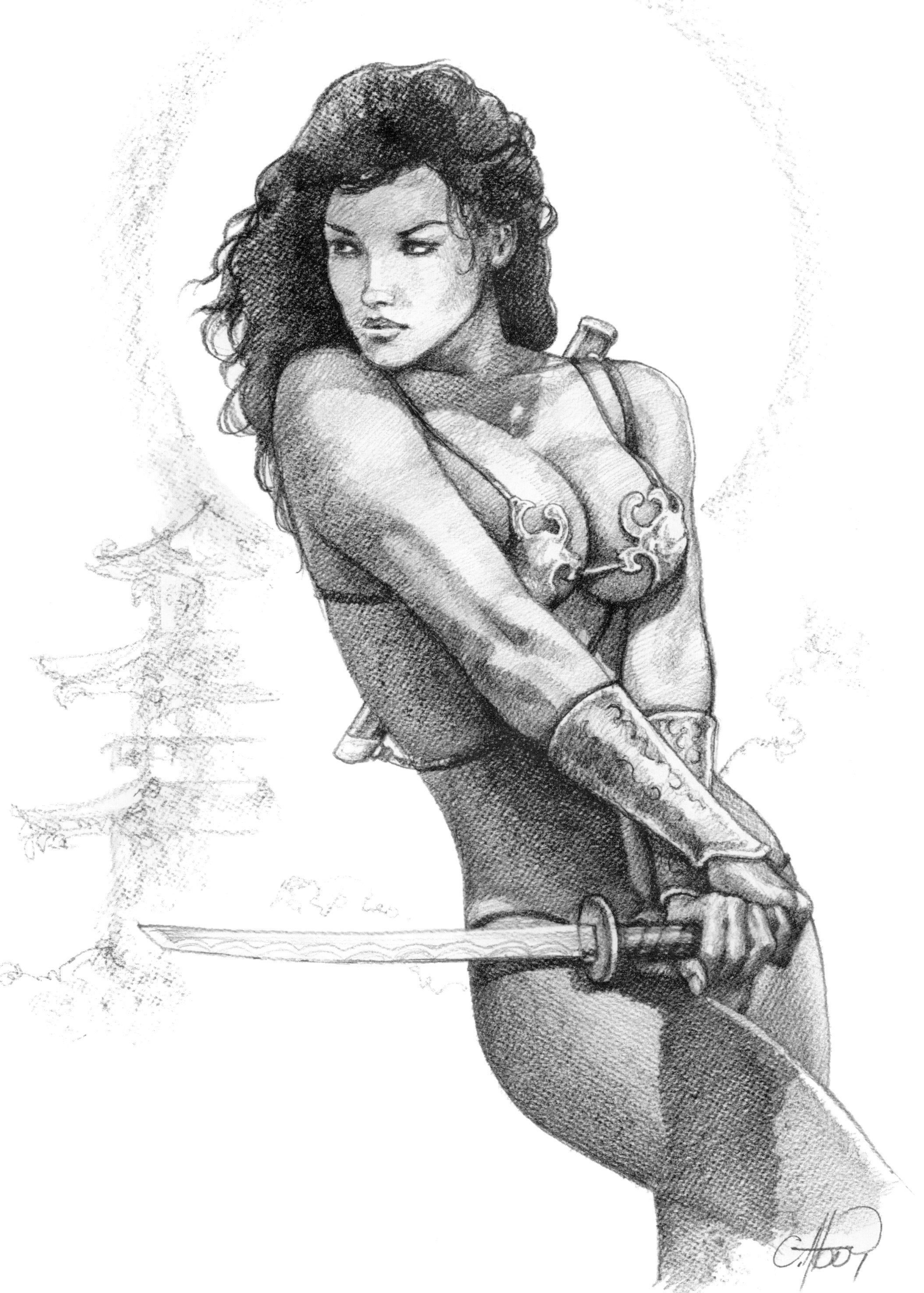

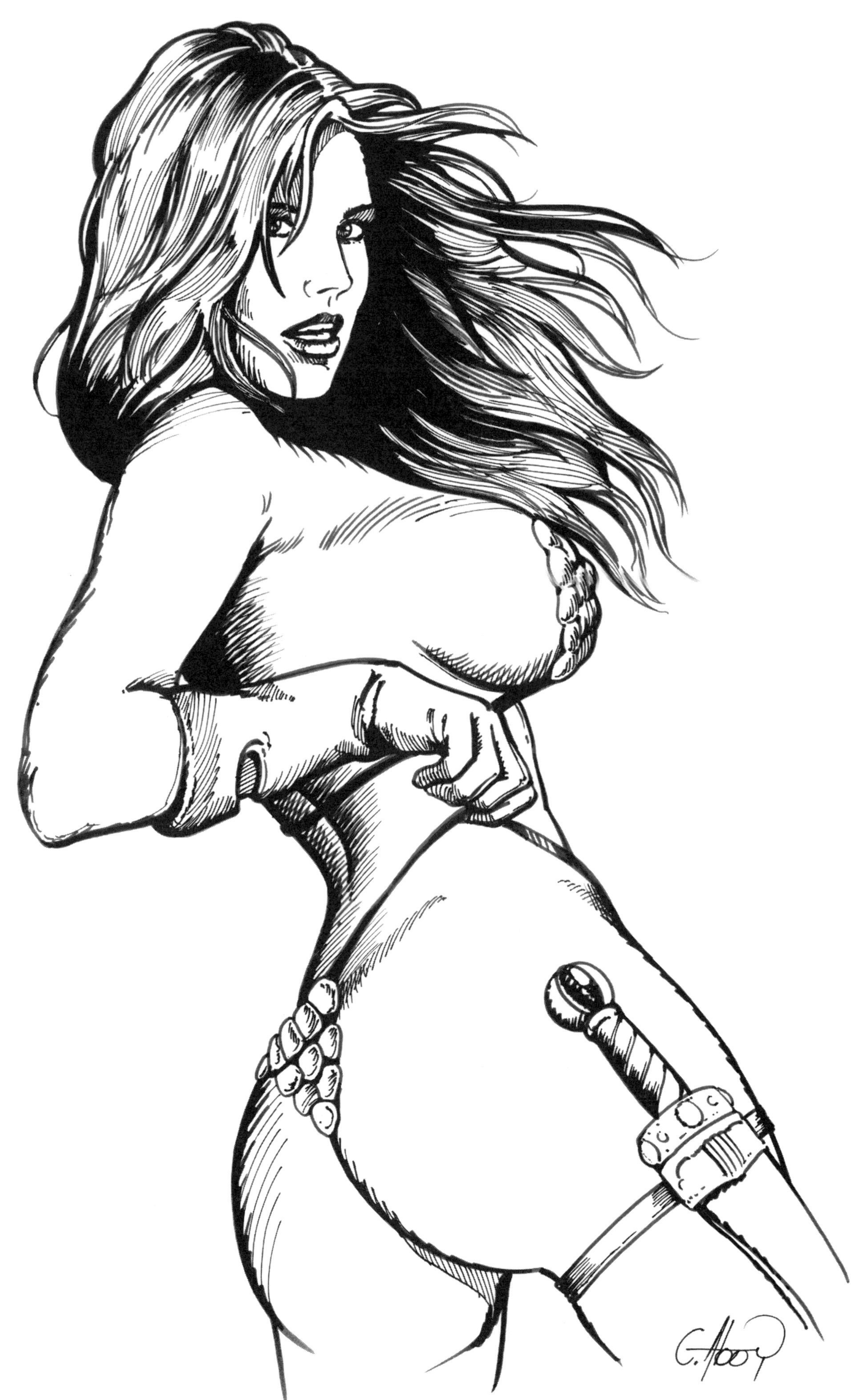

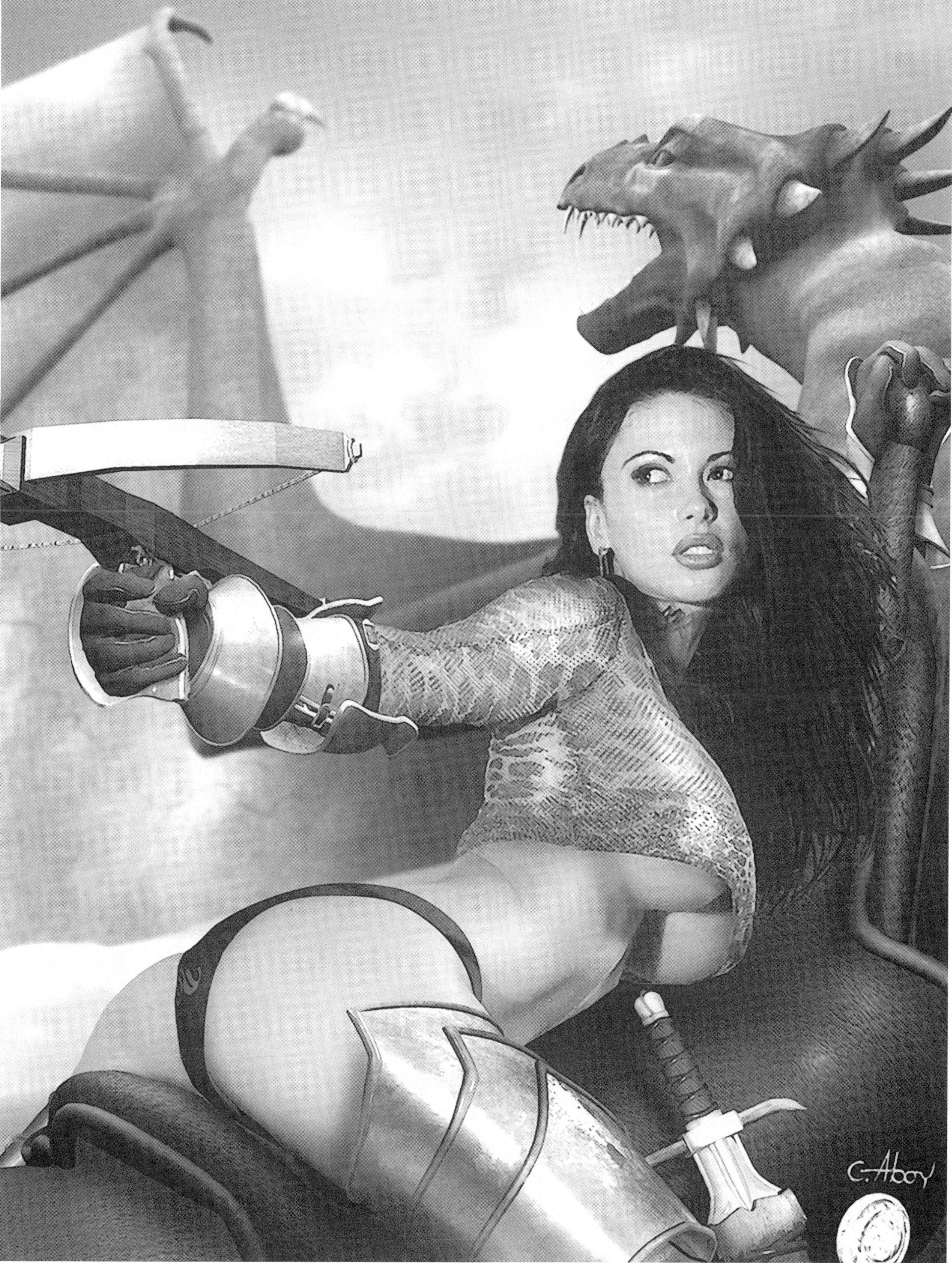
C. Aboy

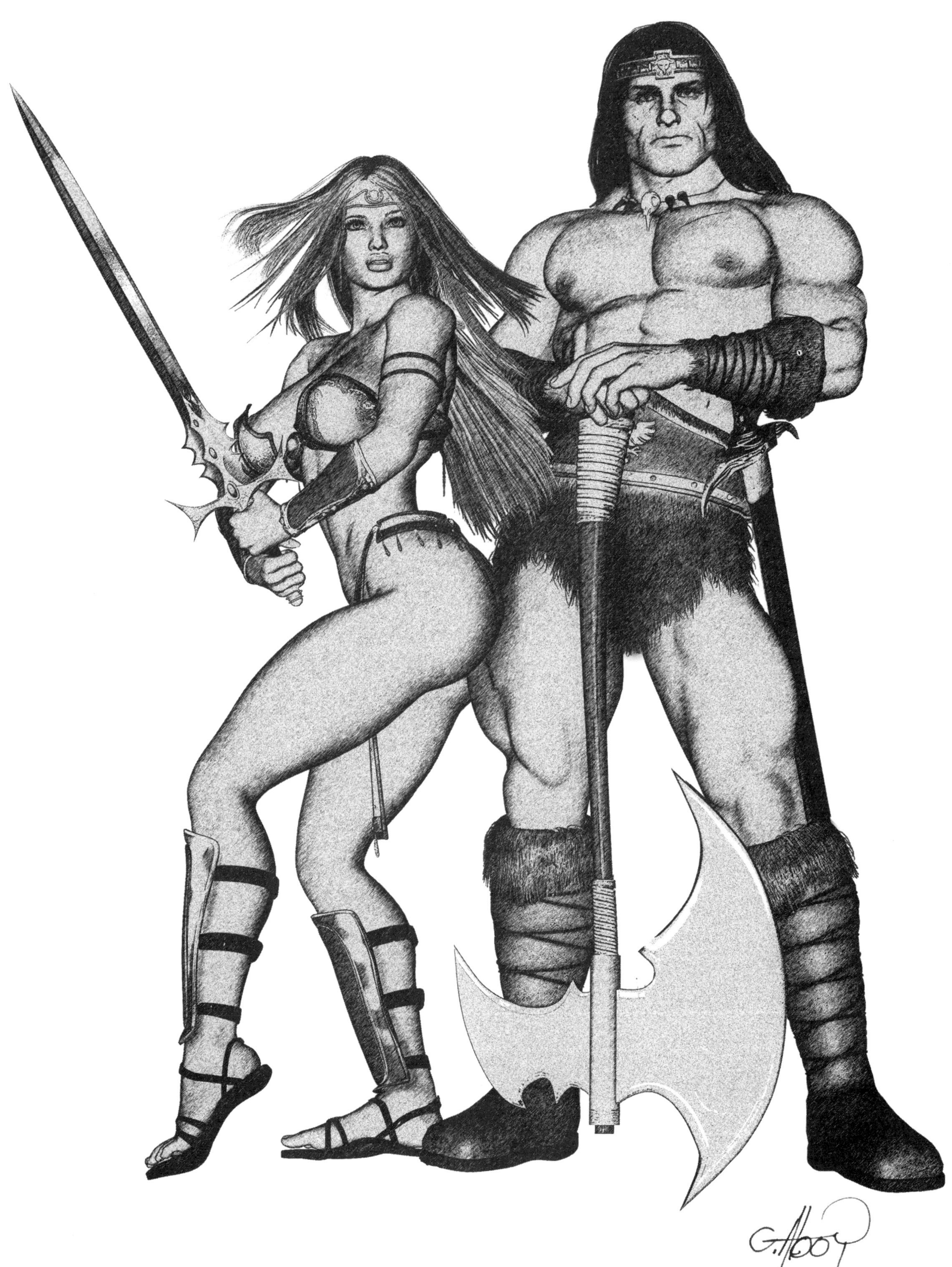

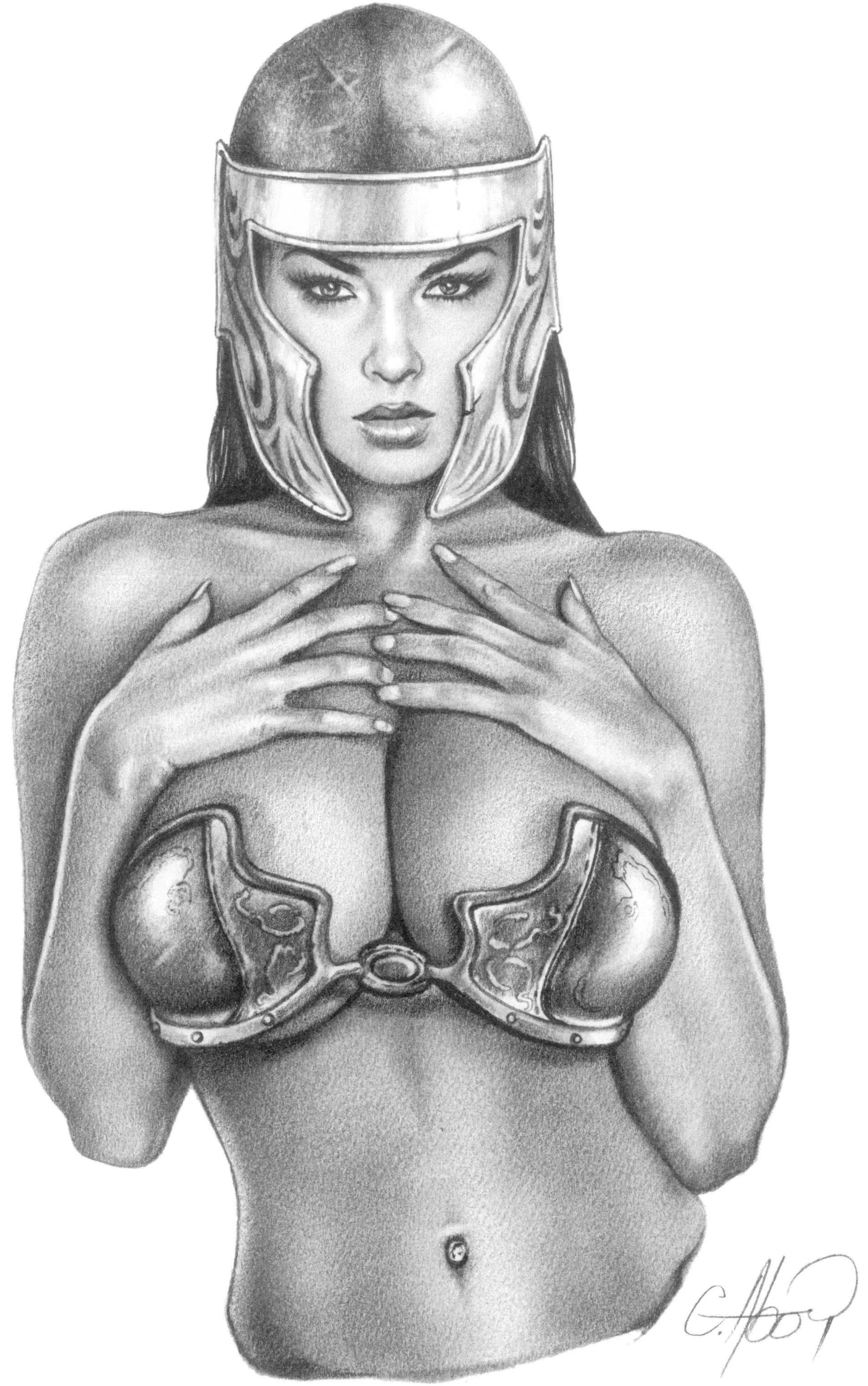

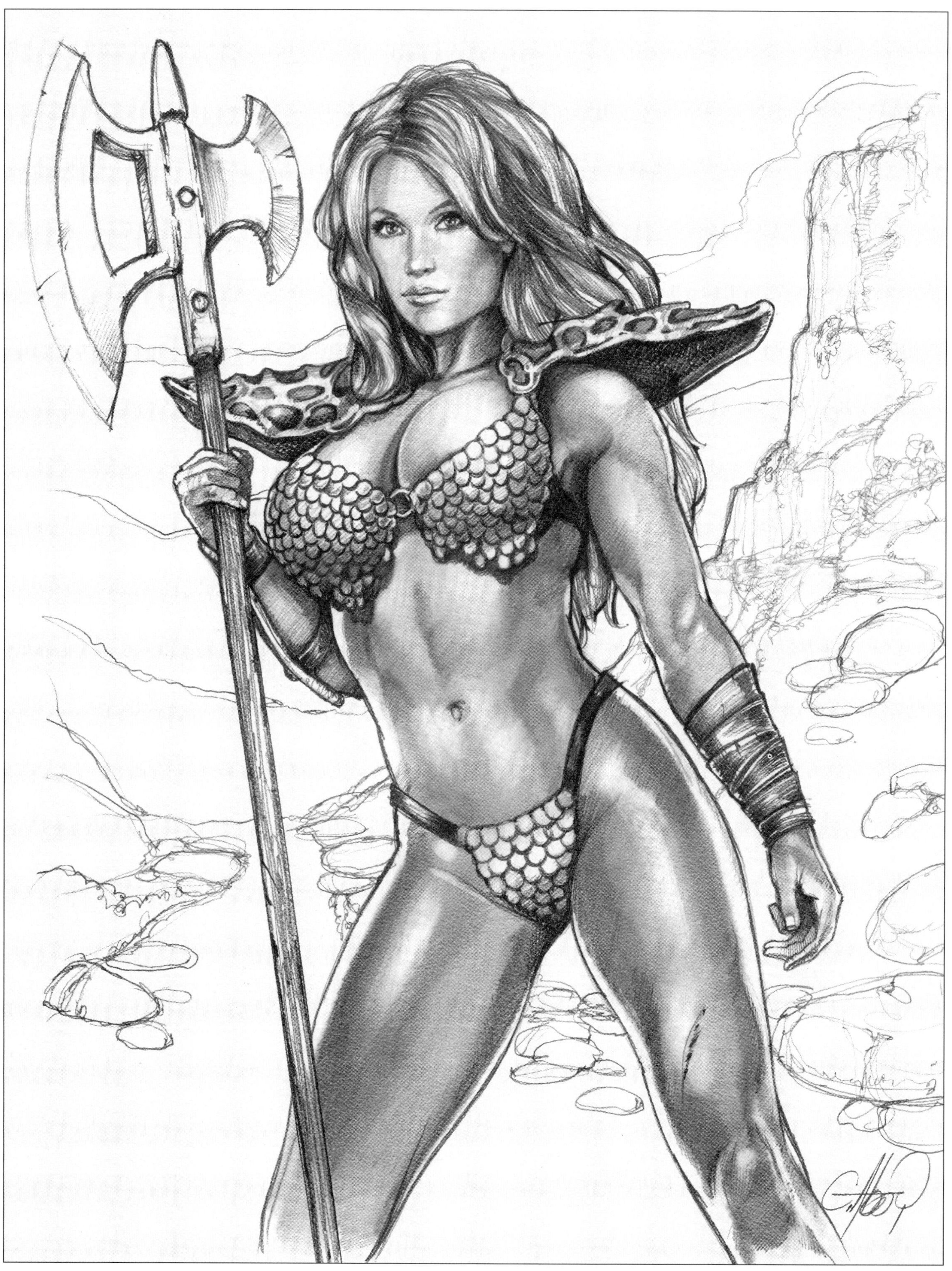

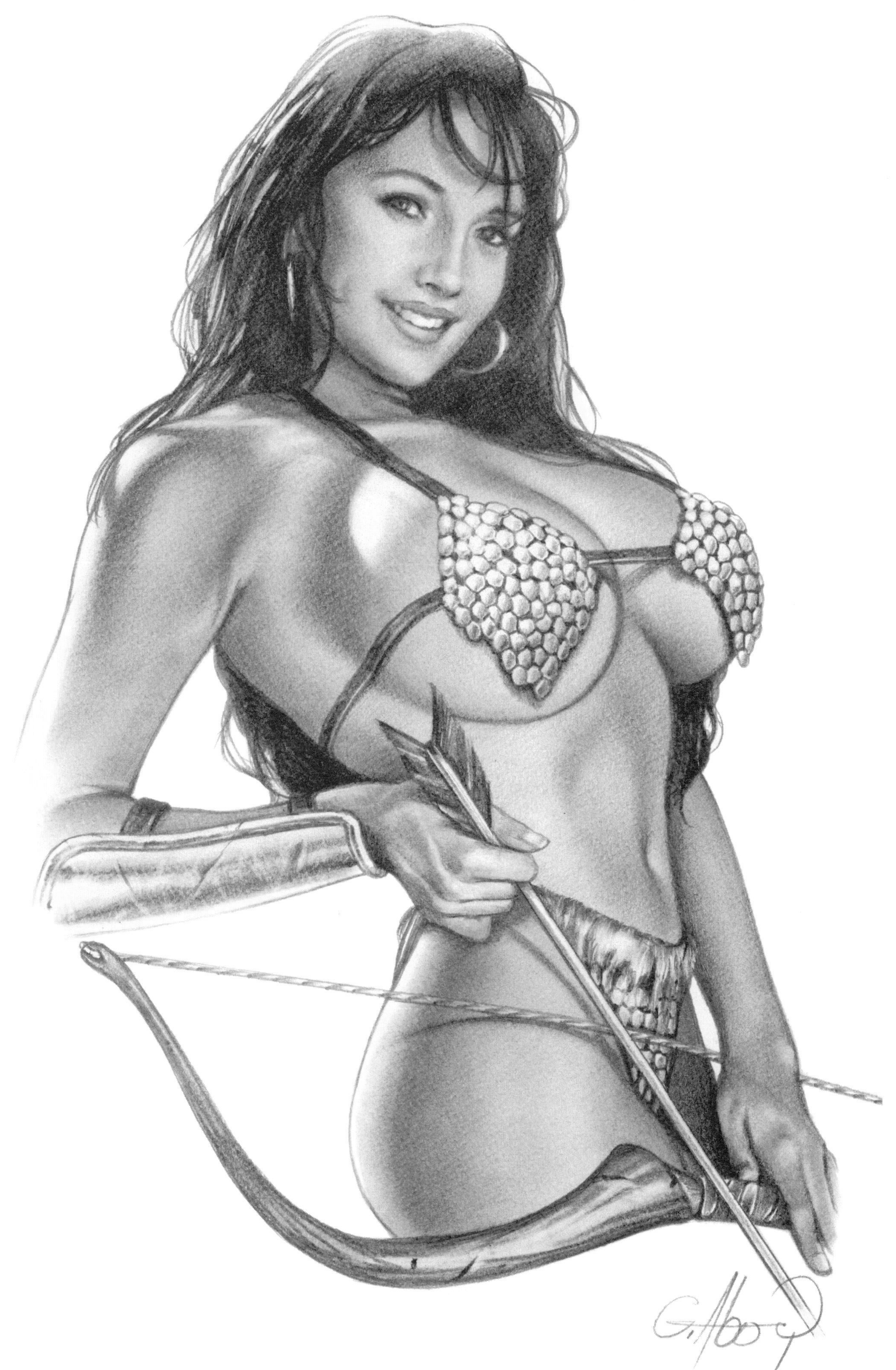

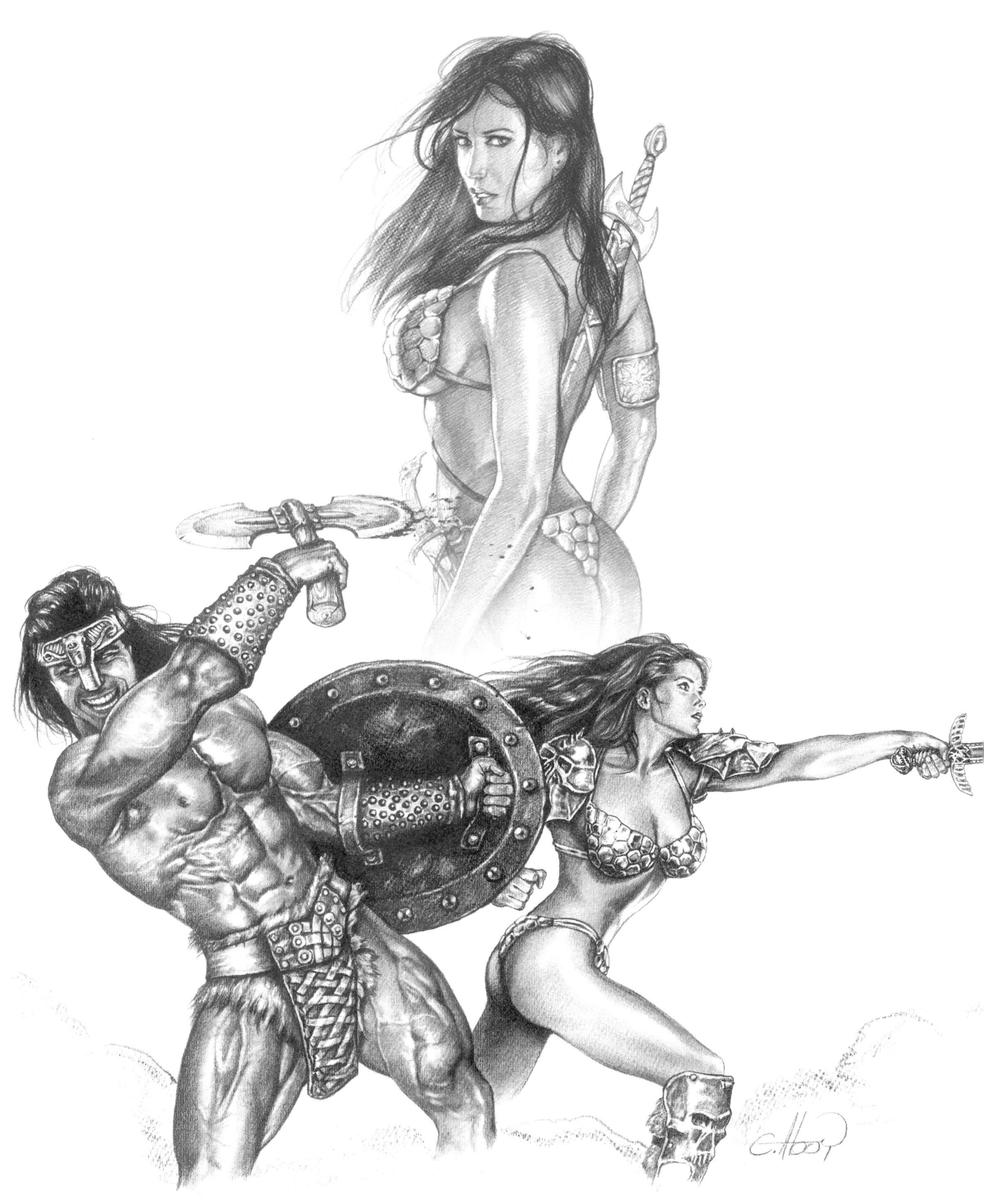

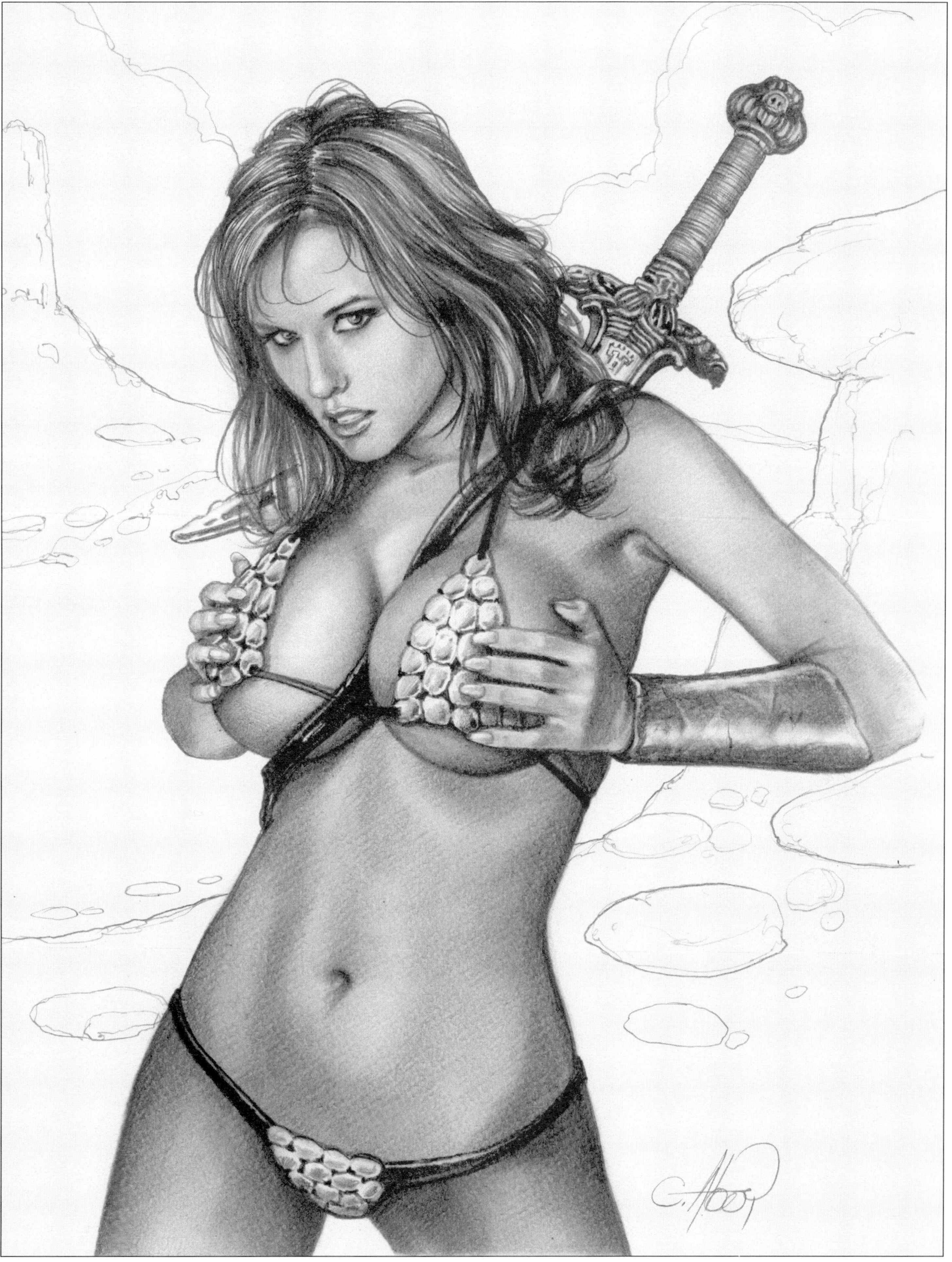

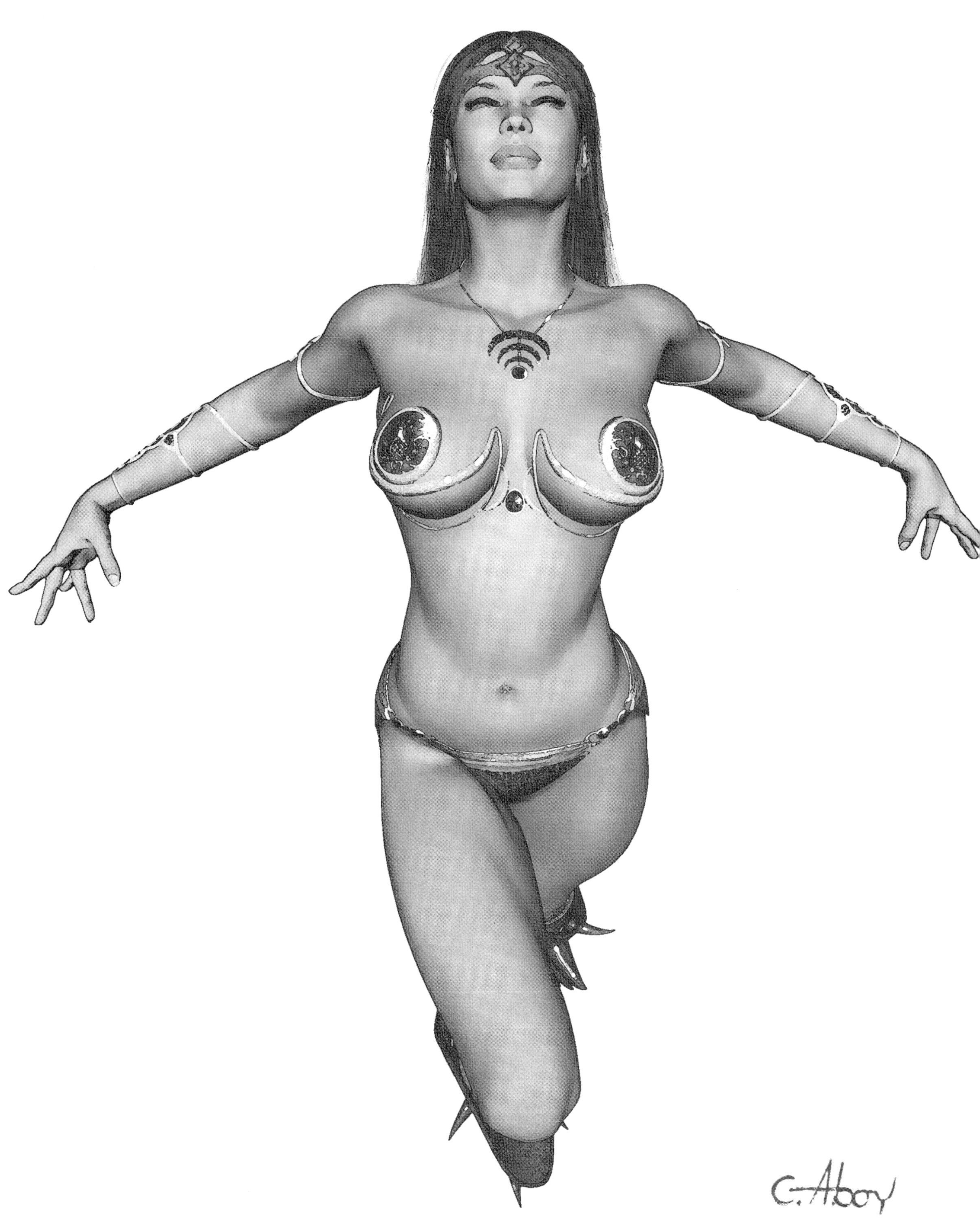
C. Aboy

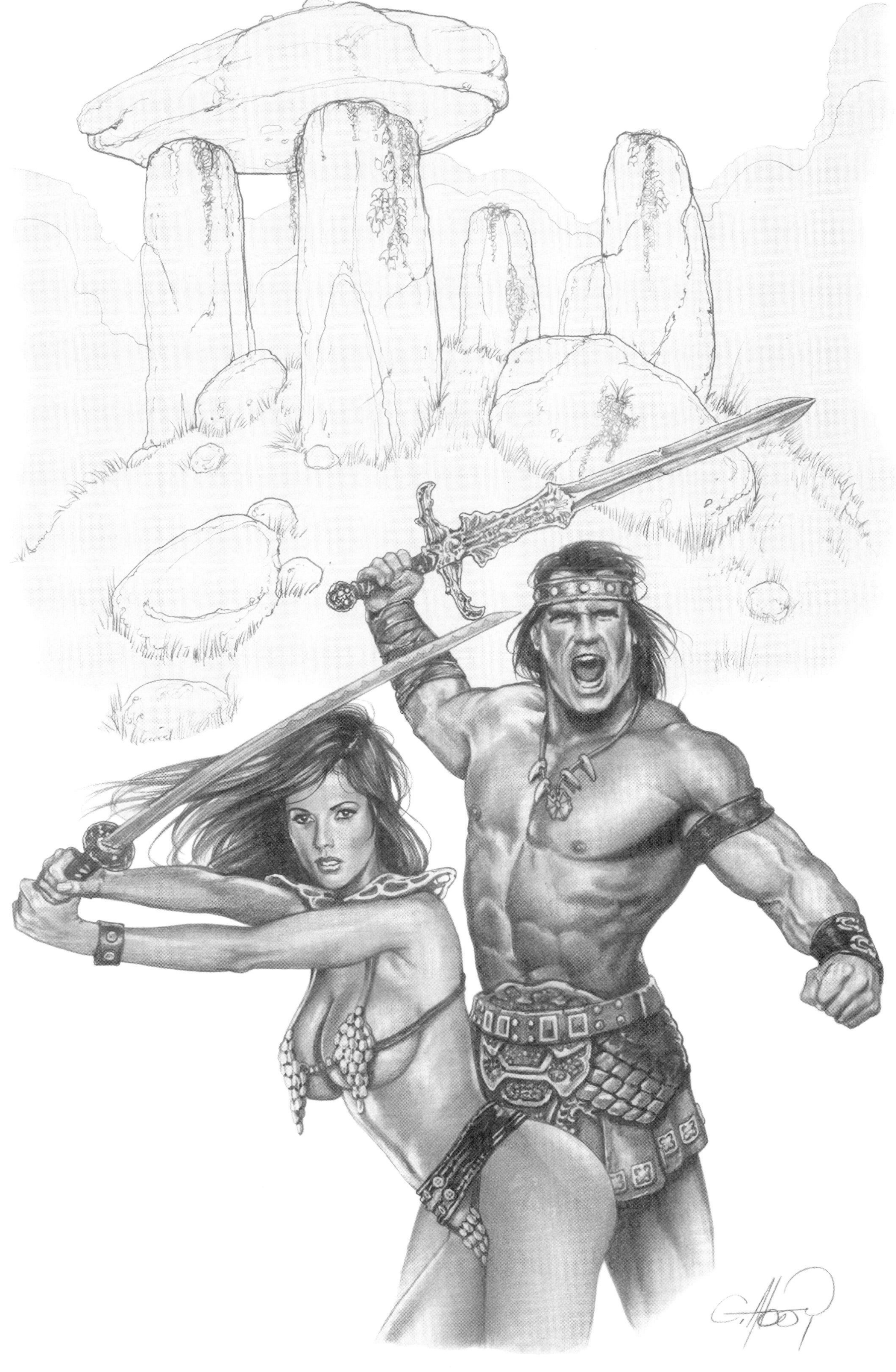

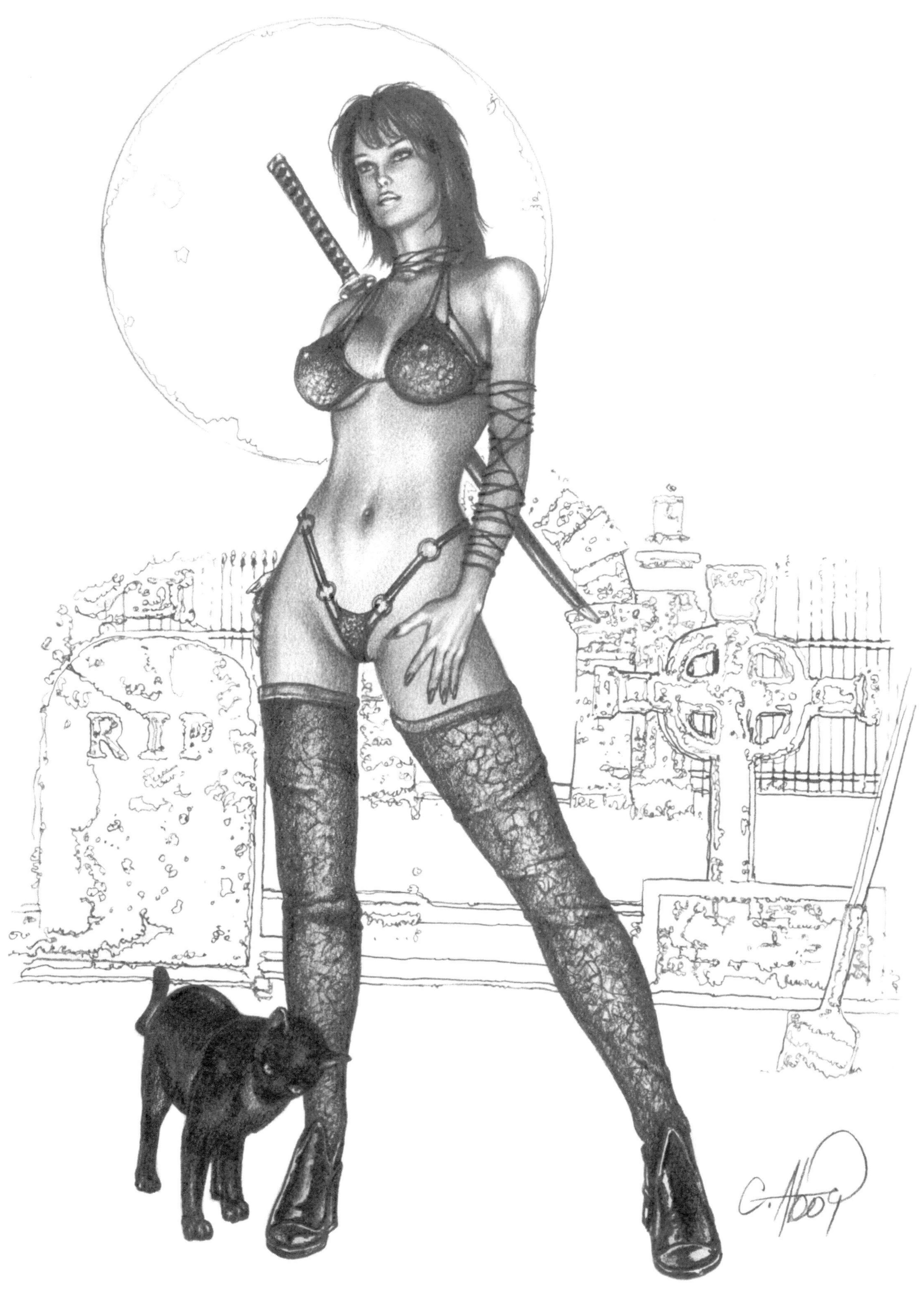
RIP

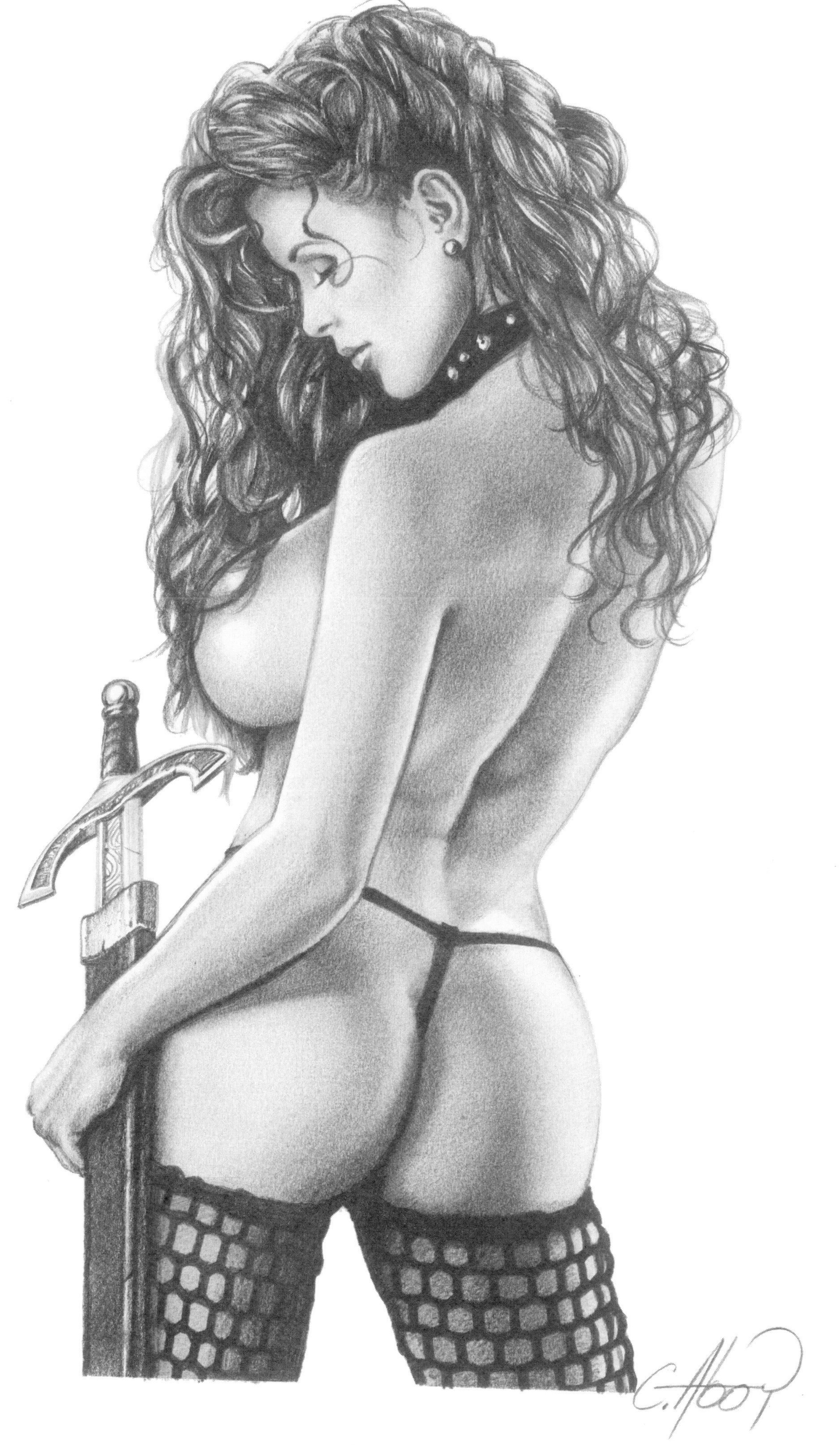

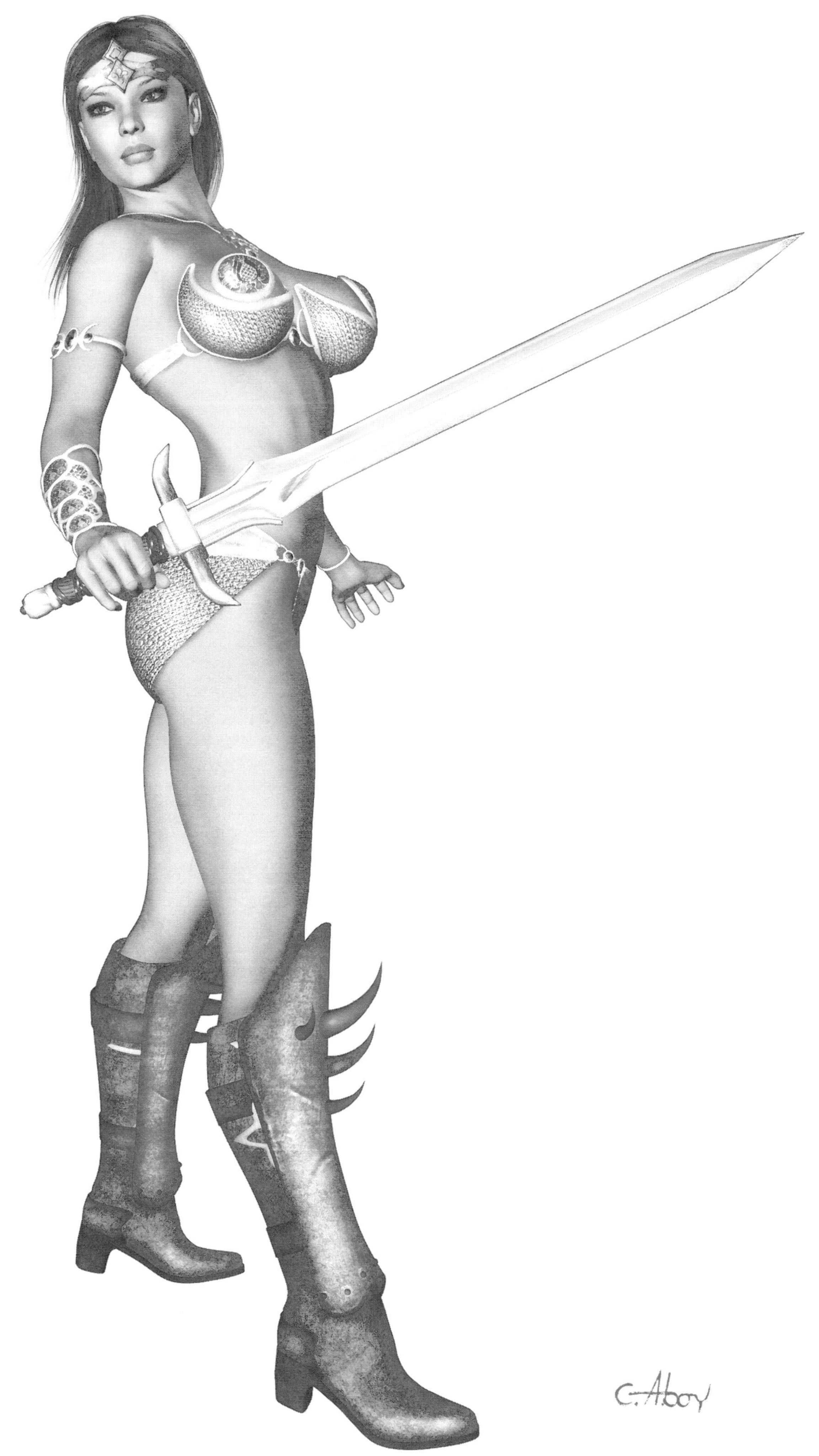
C. Aboy

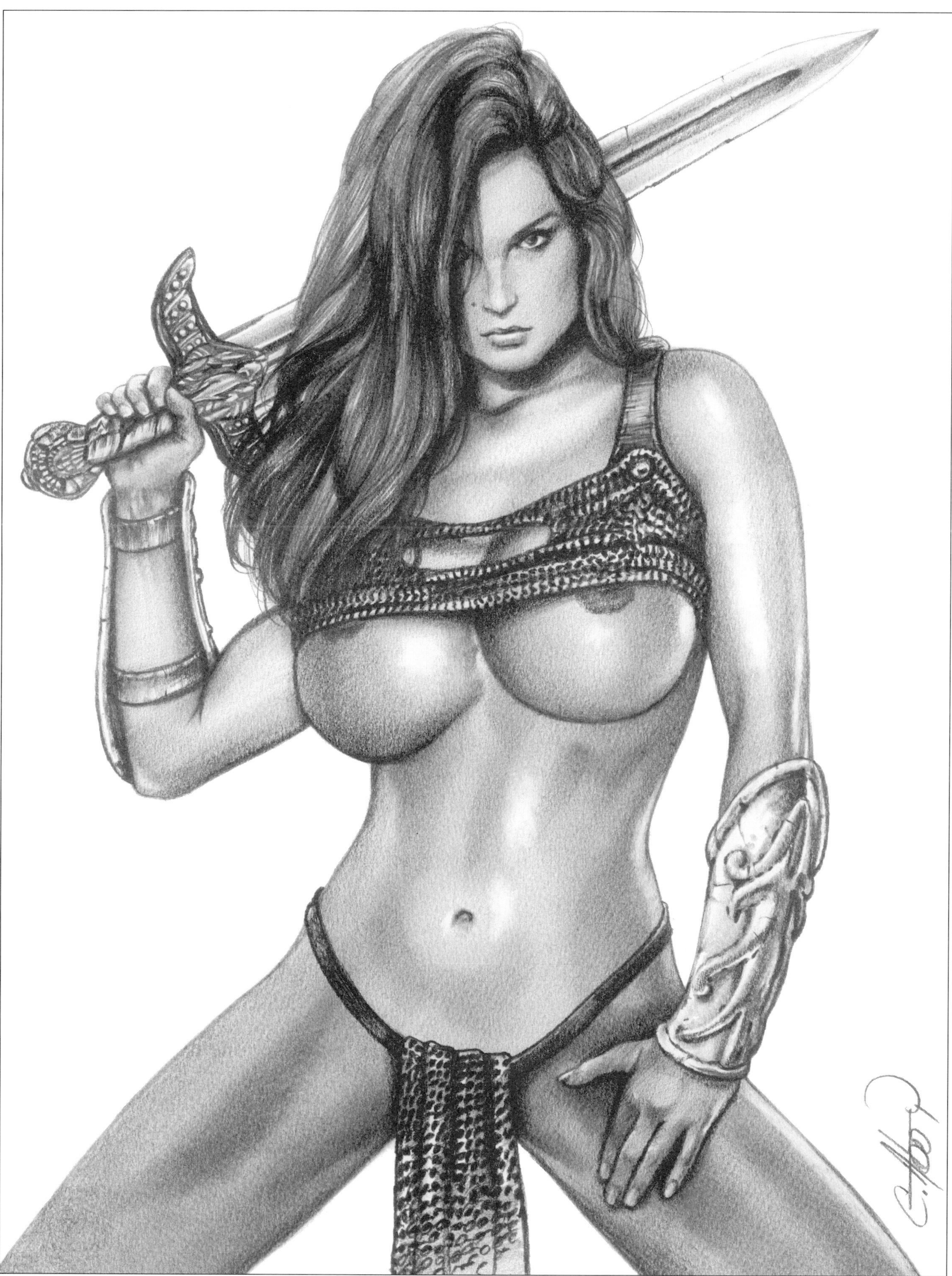

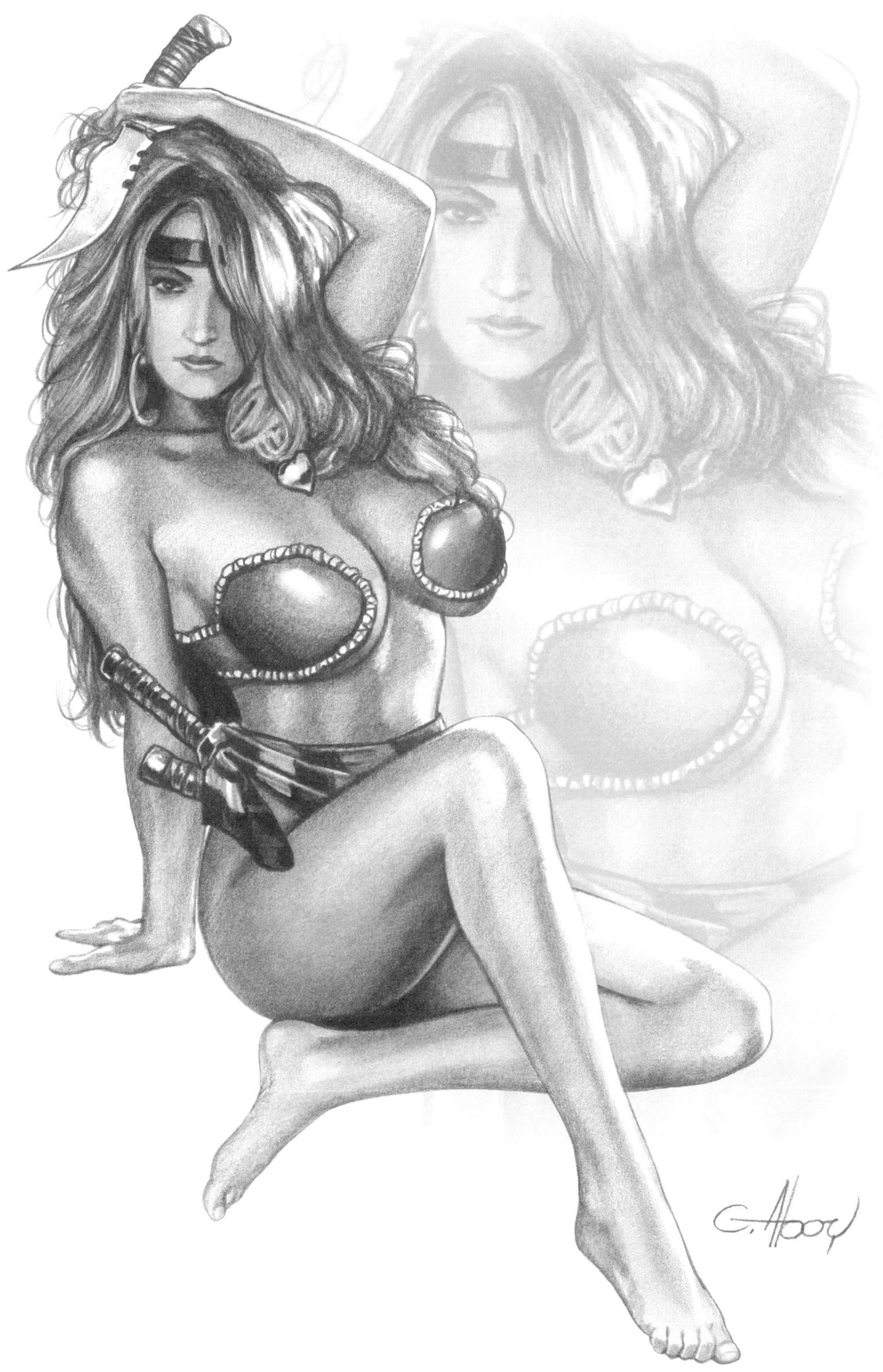

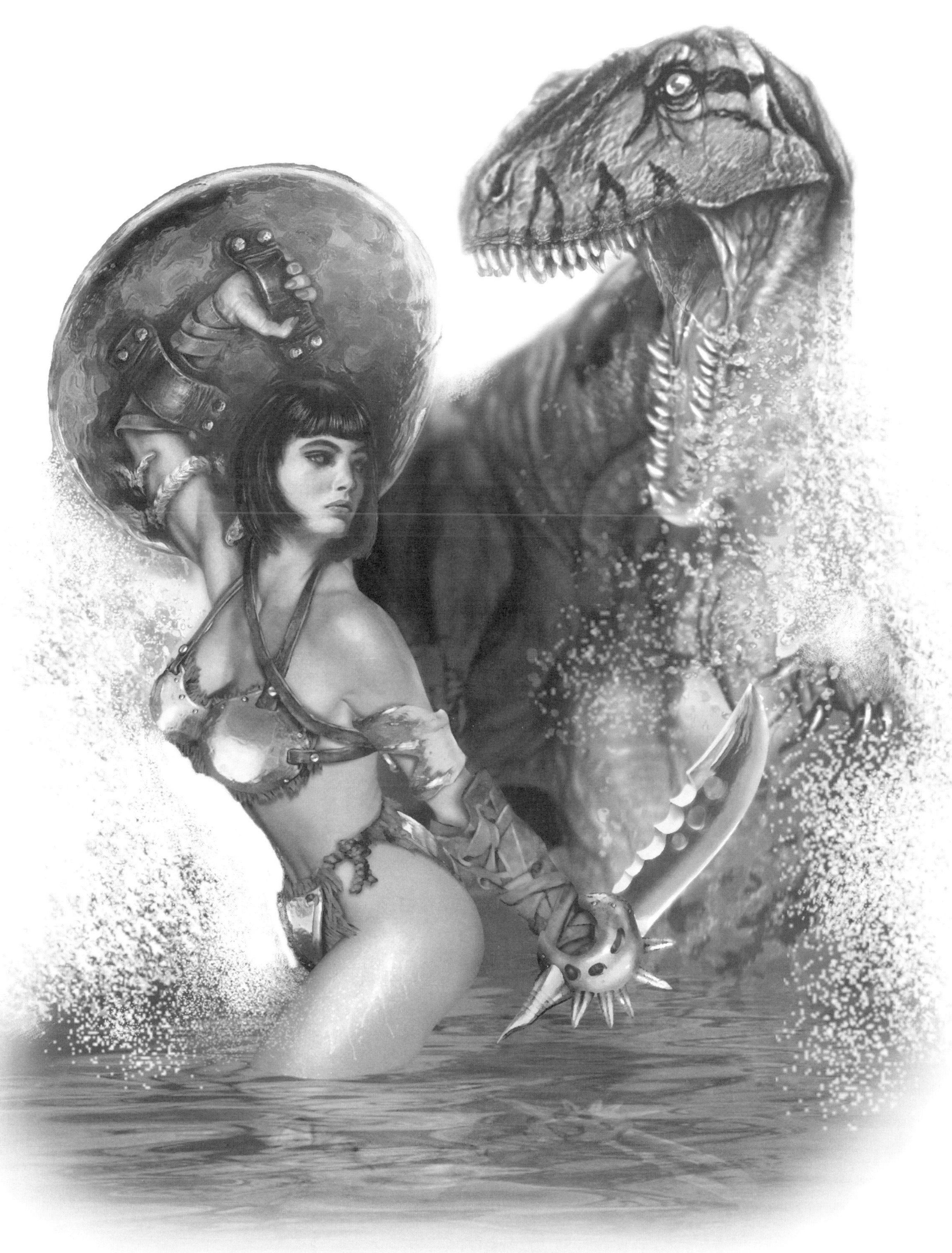

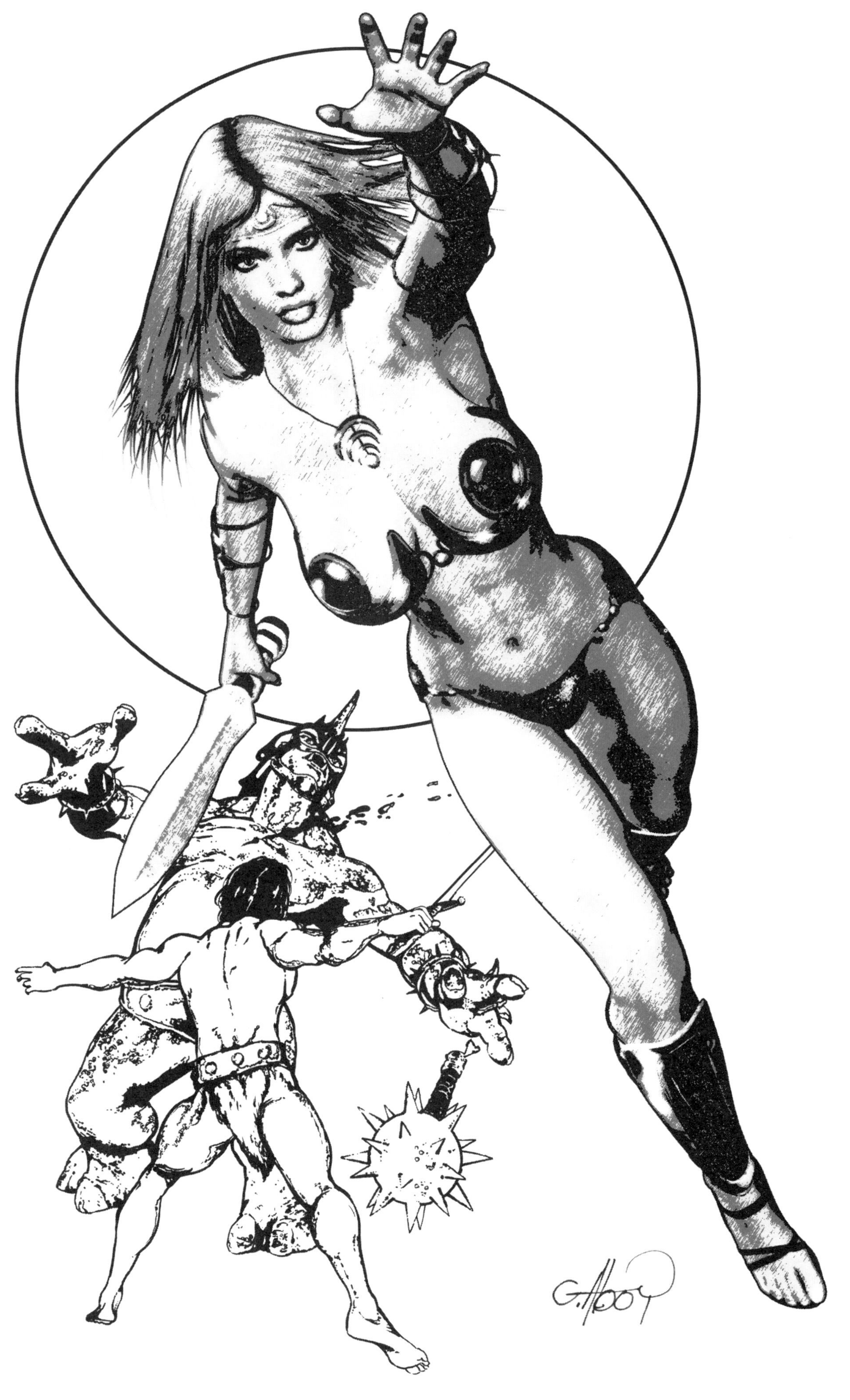

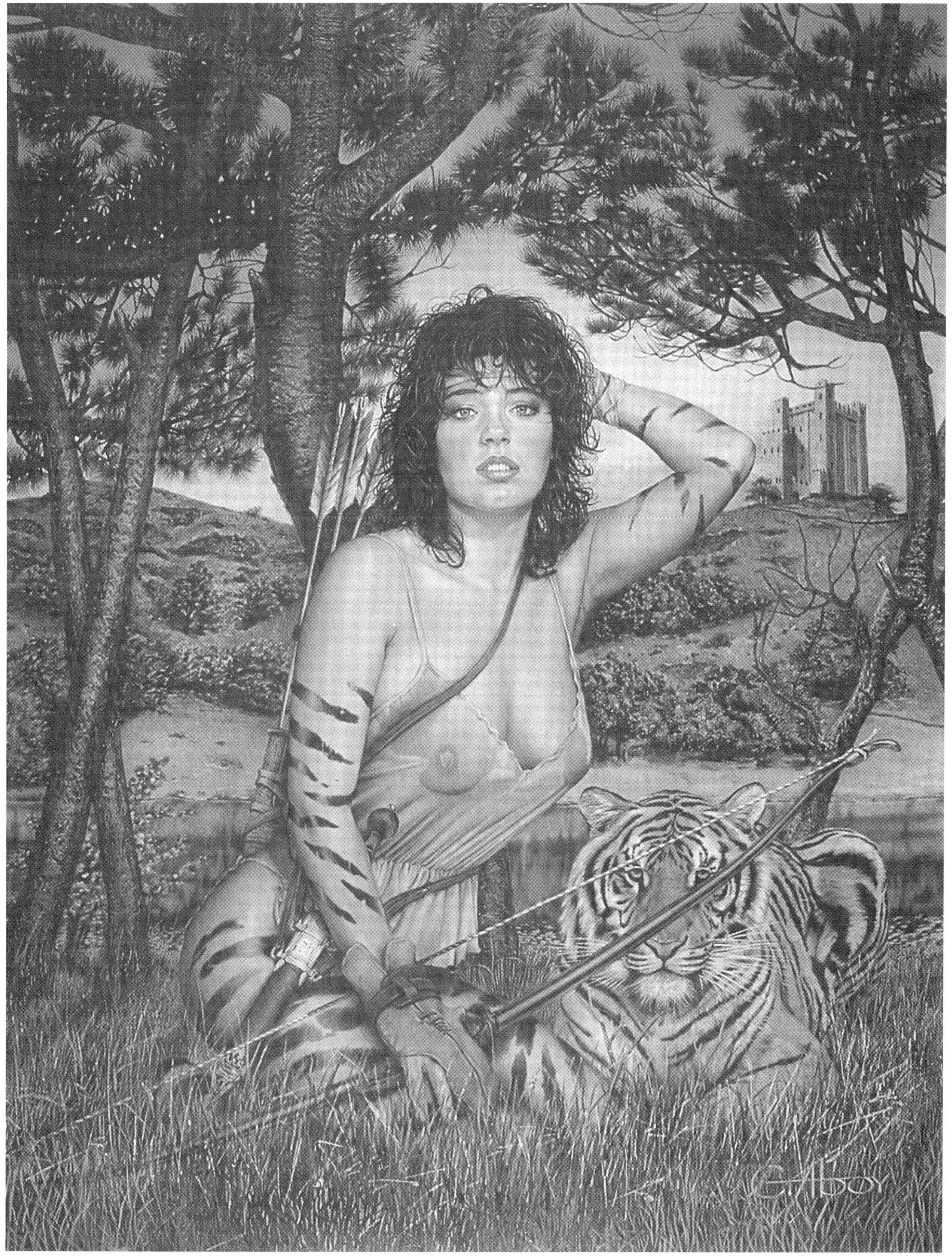

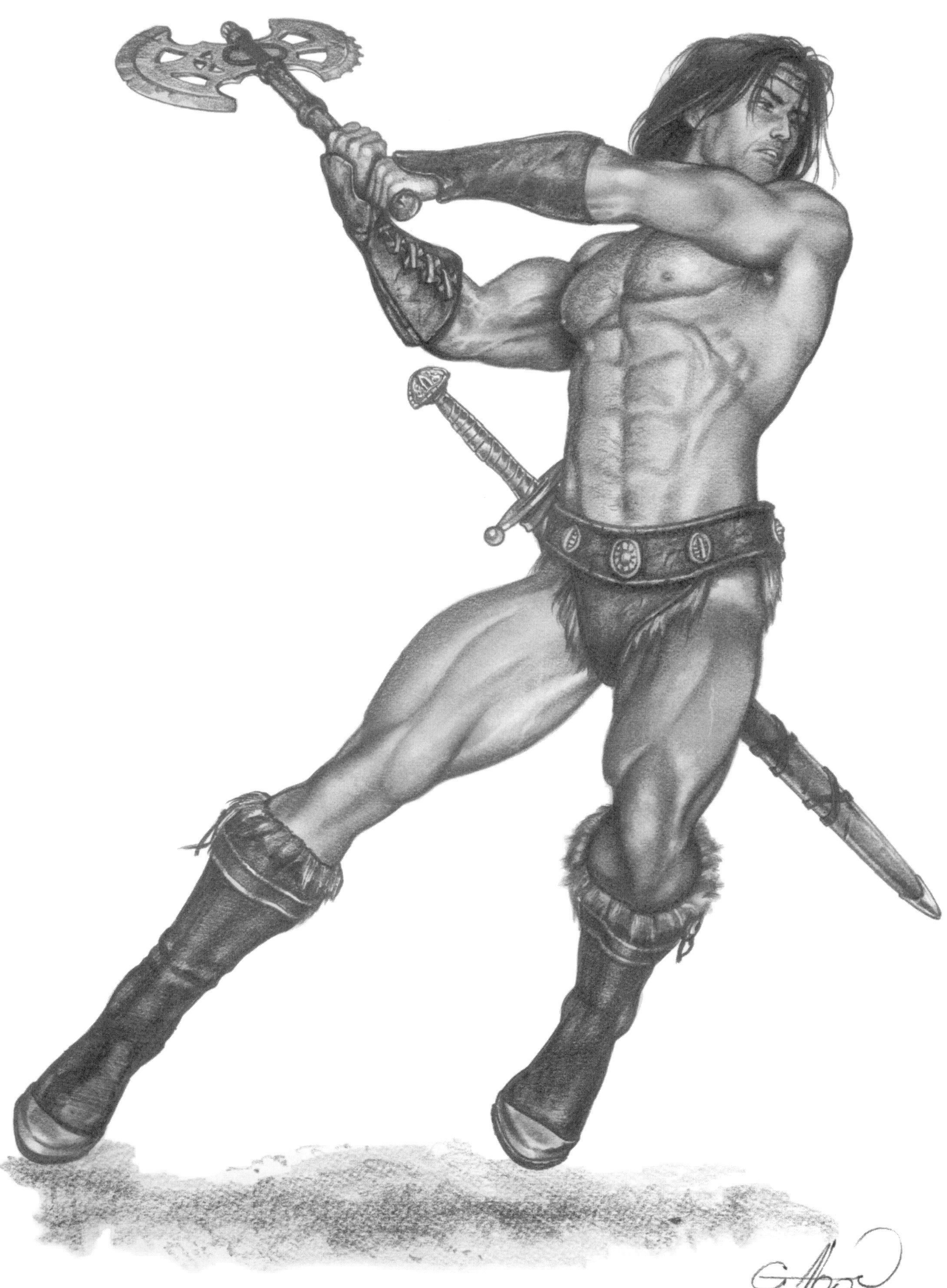

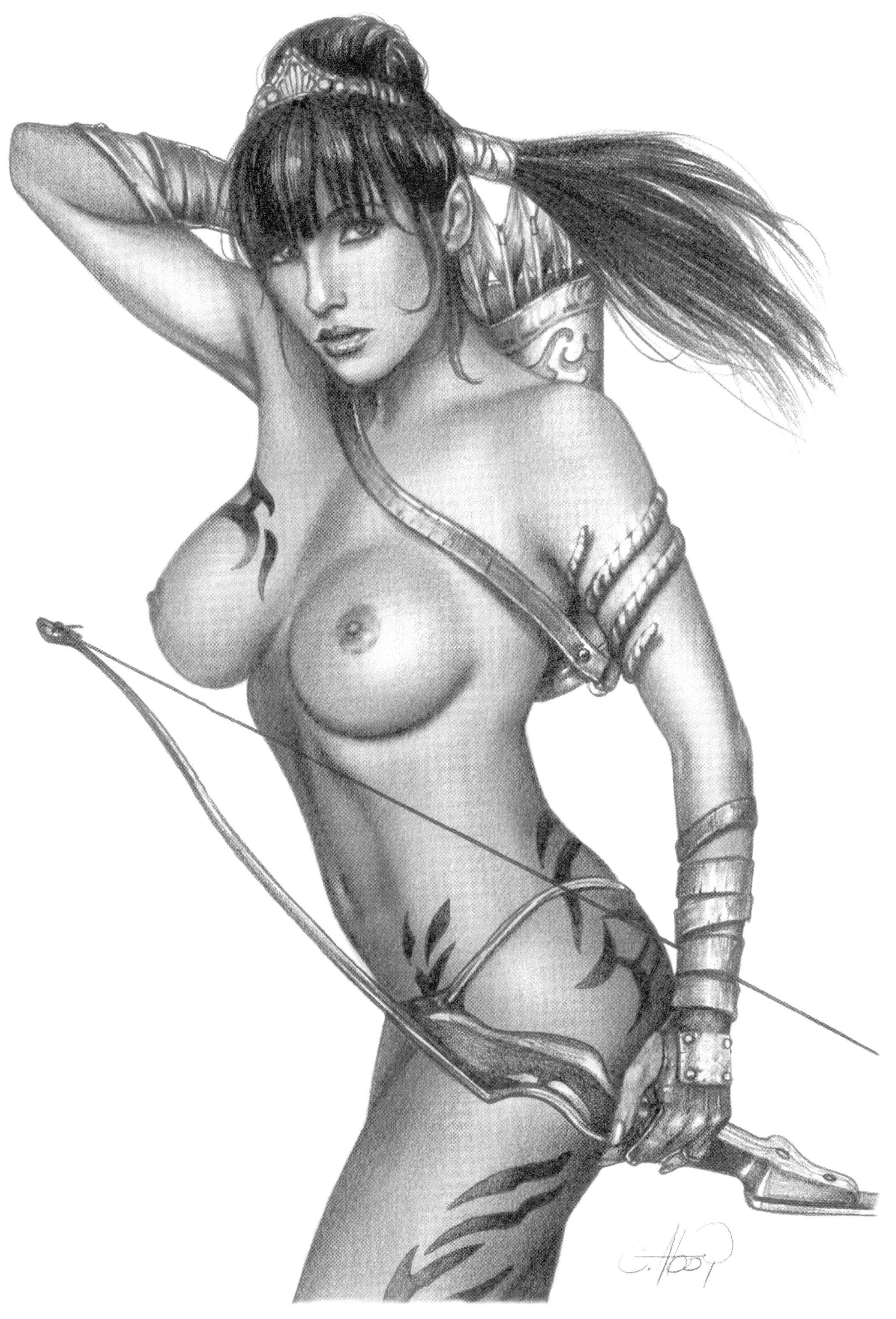

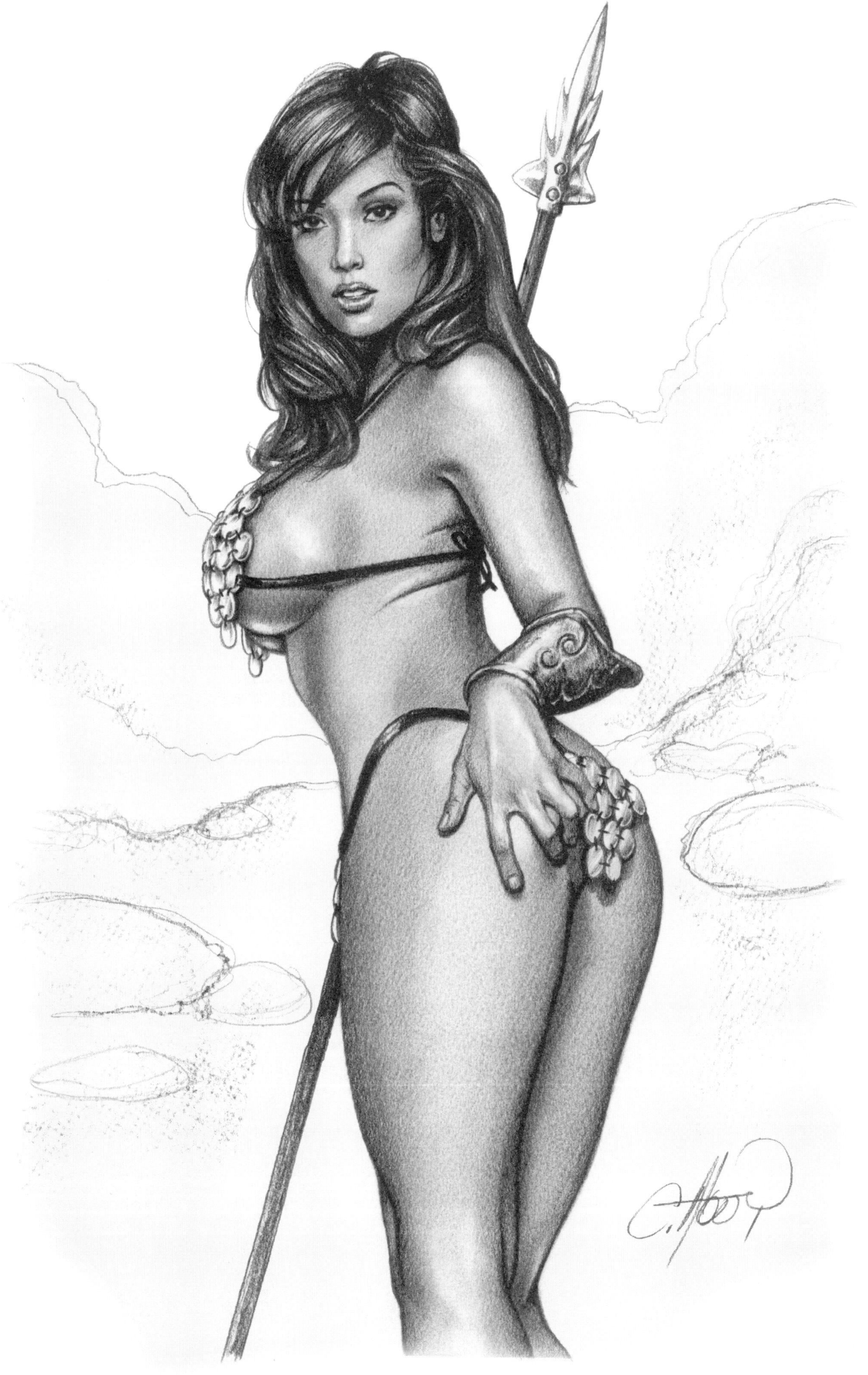

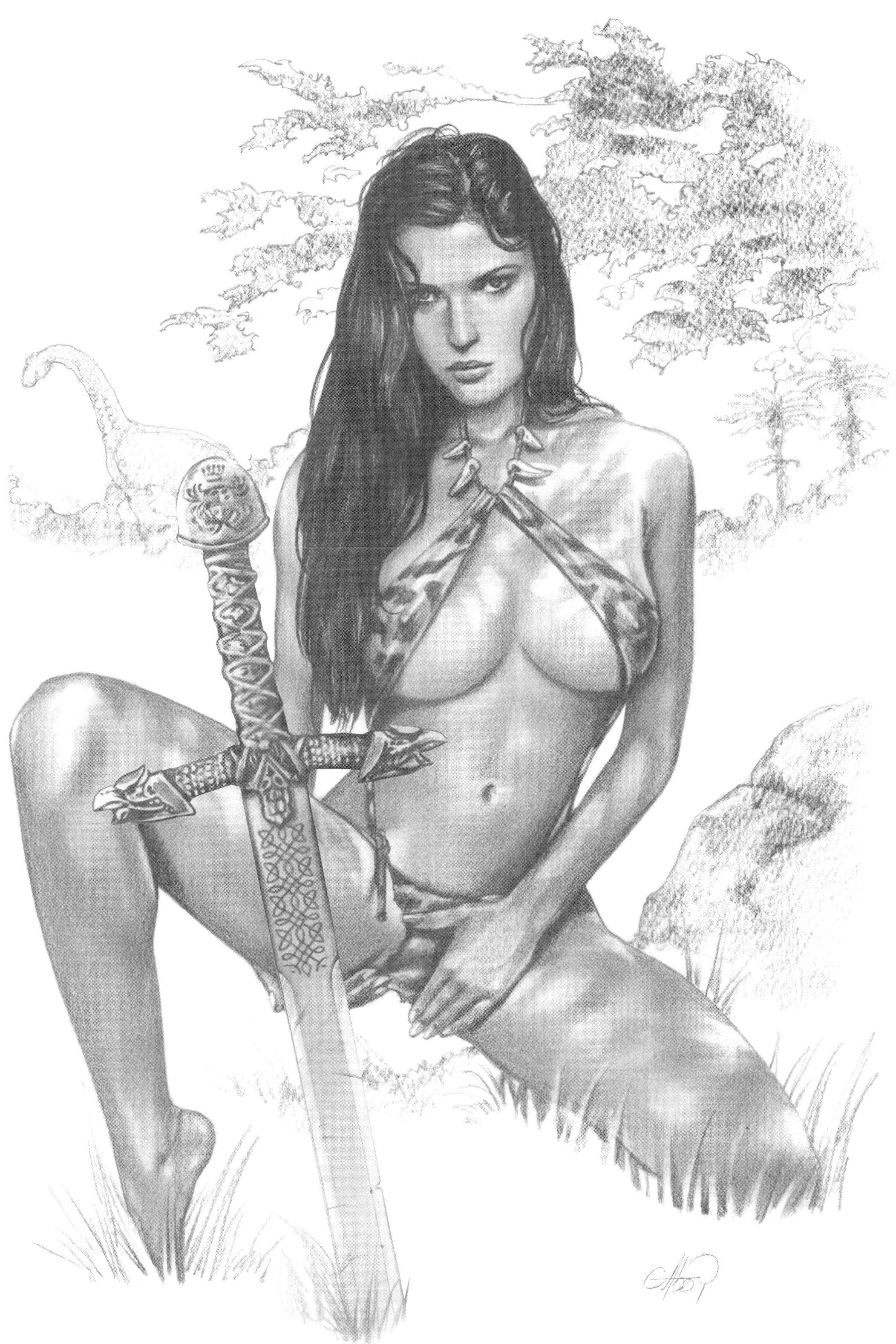

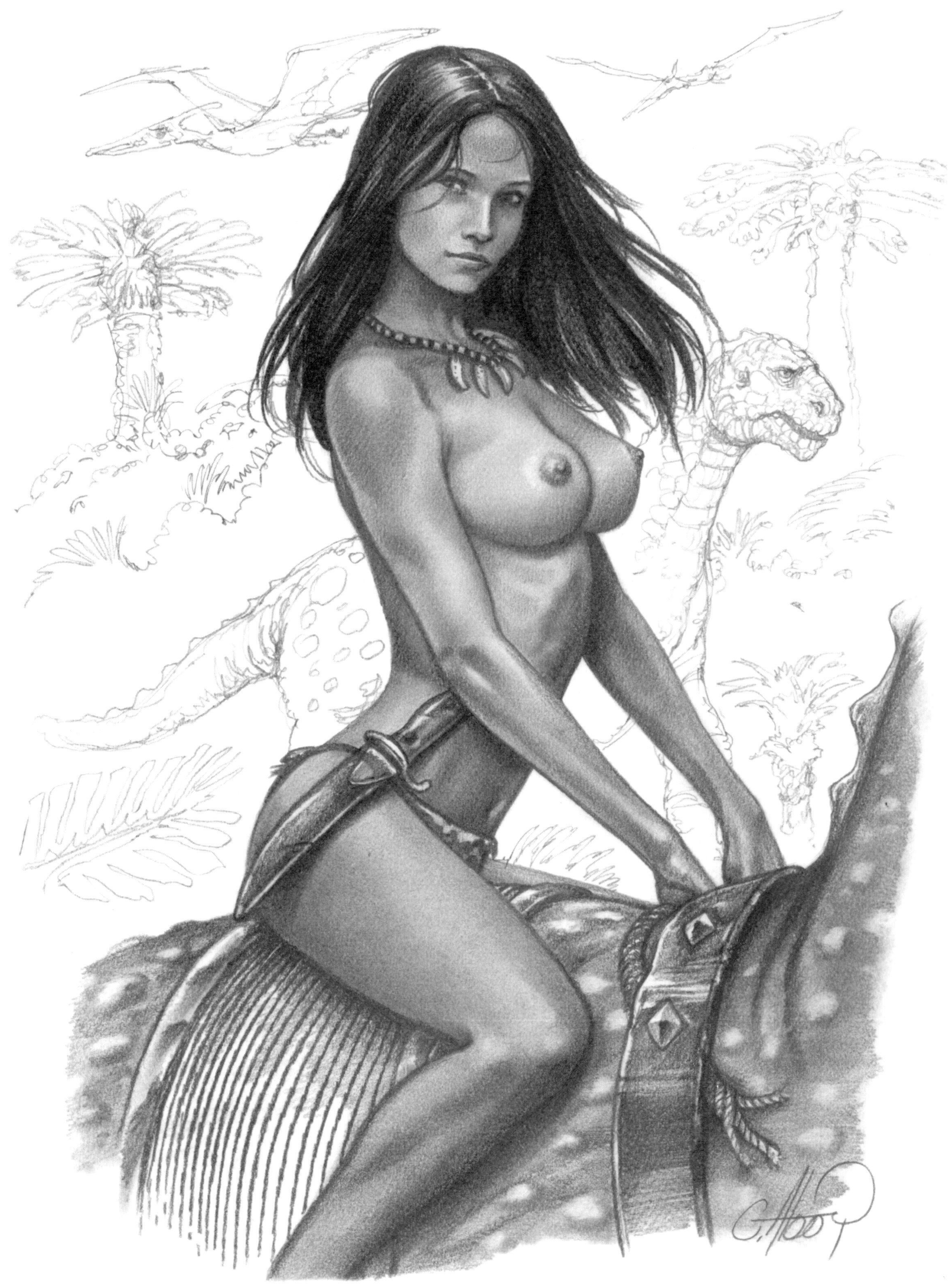

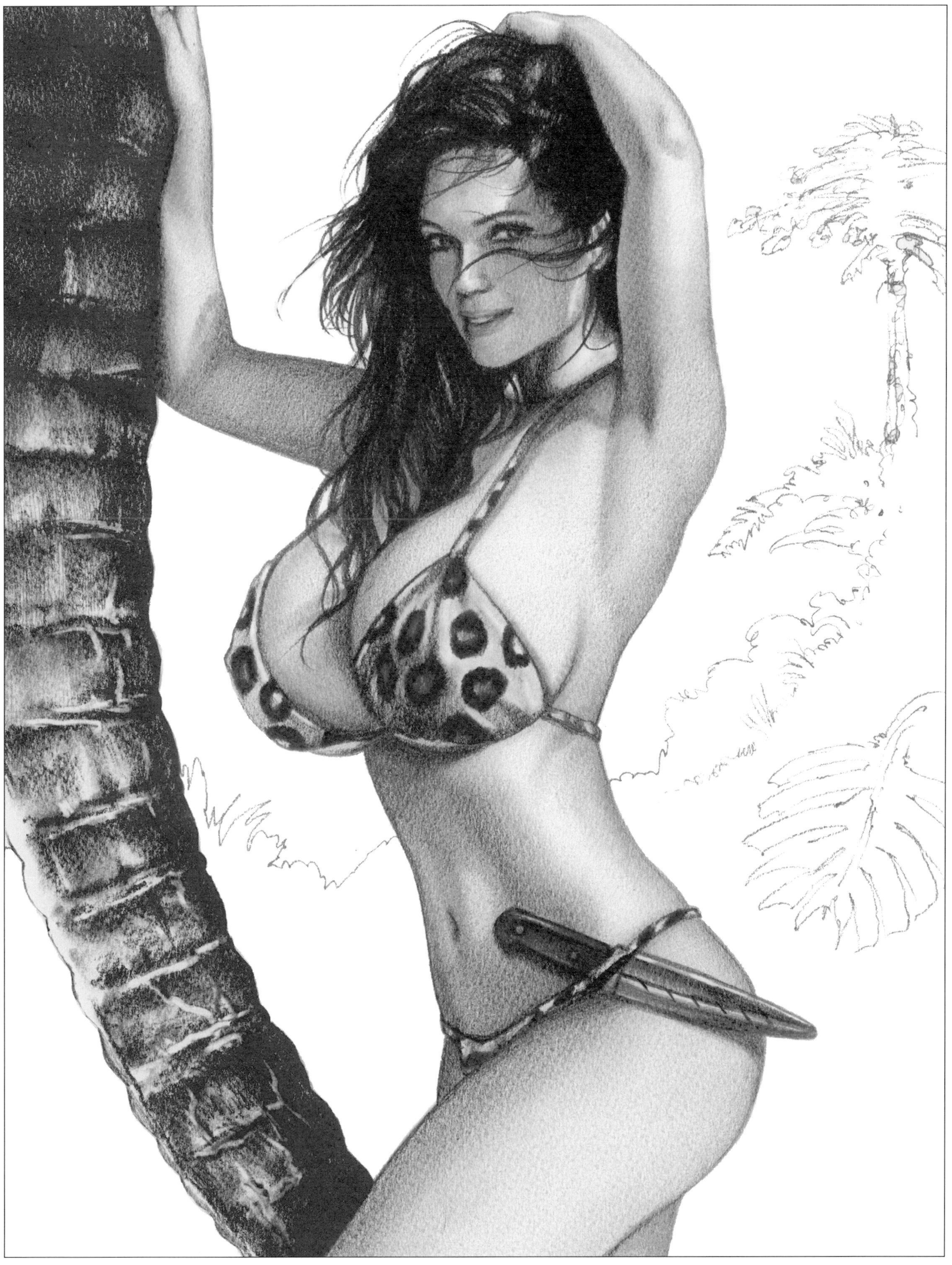

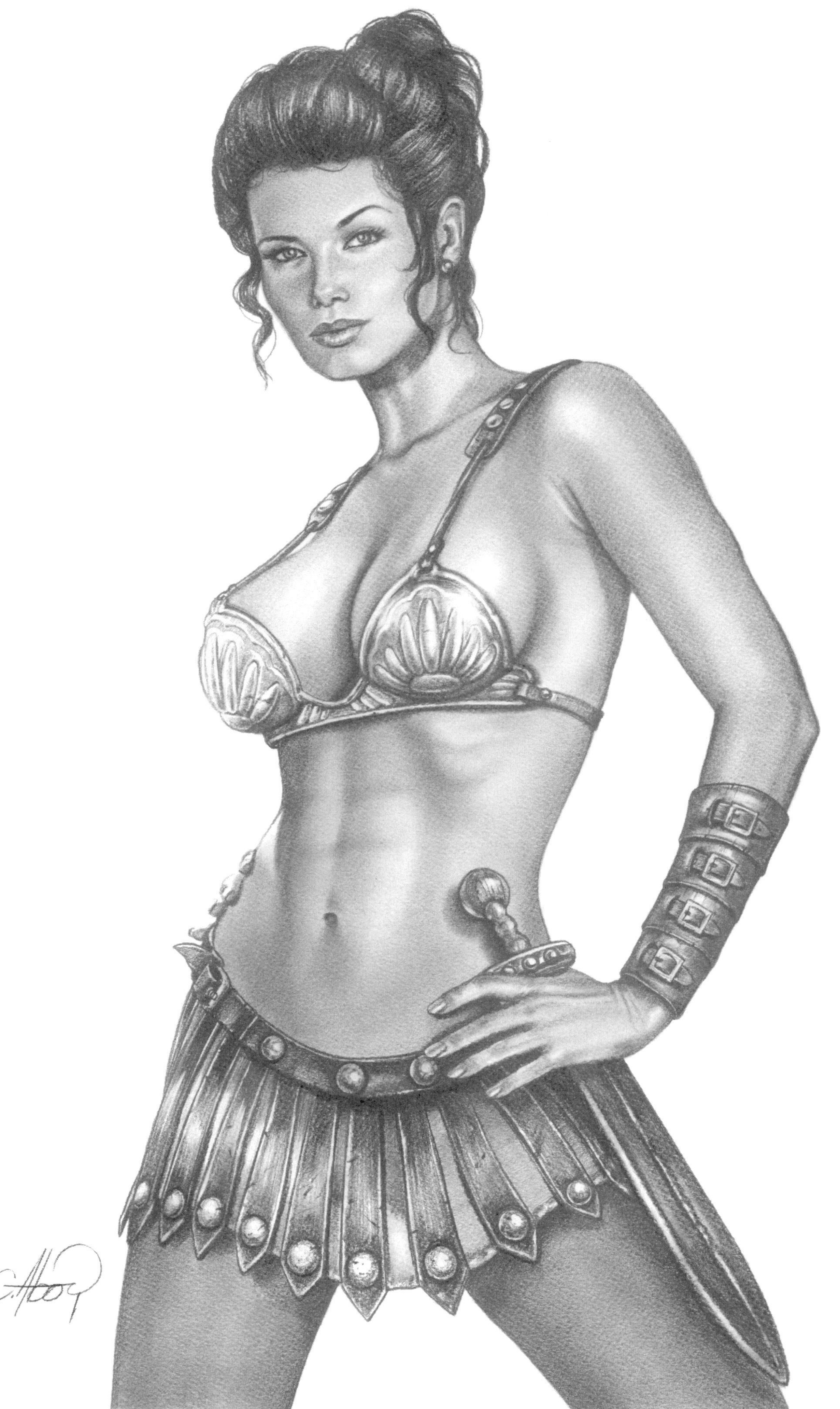

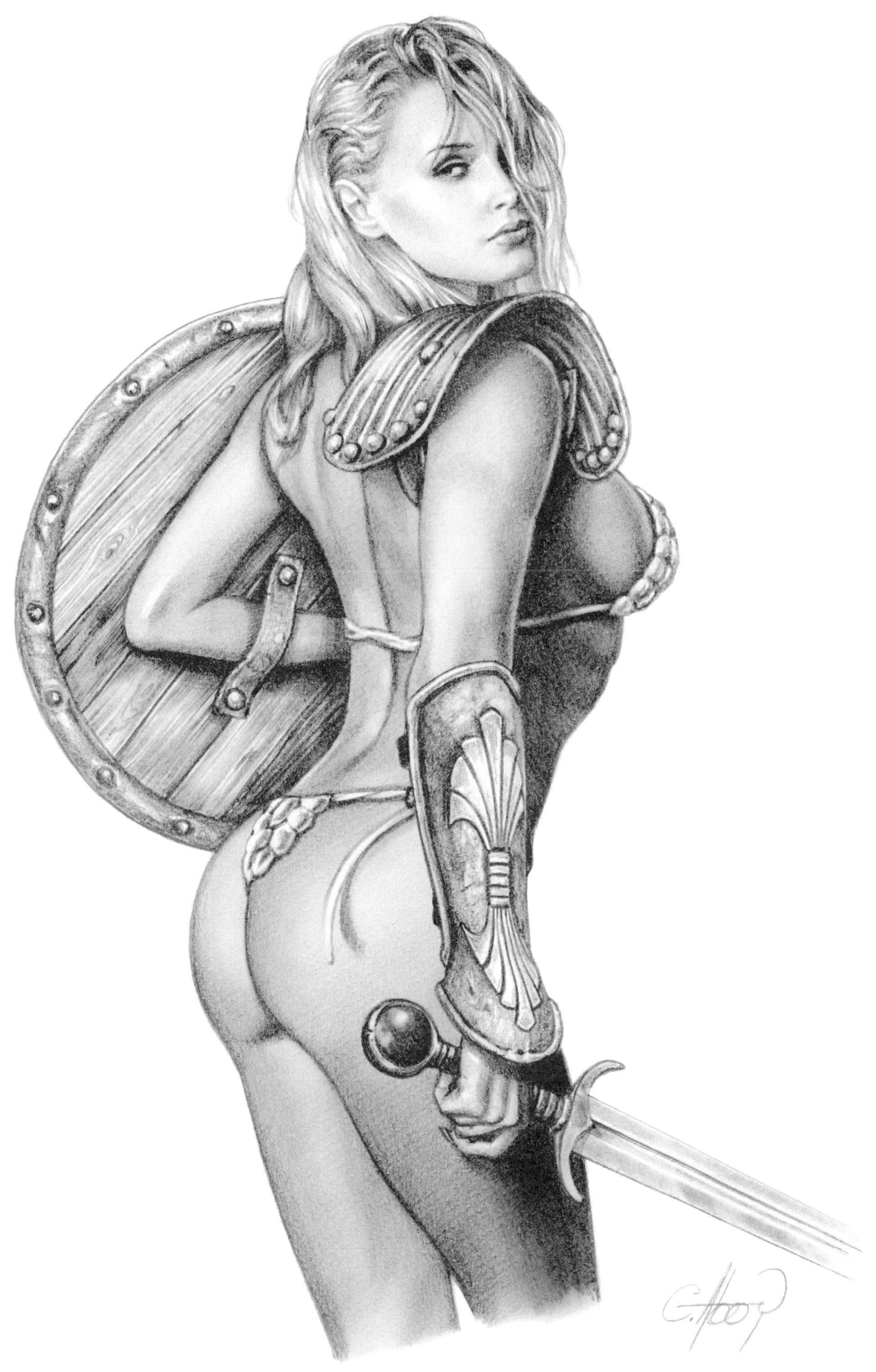

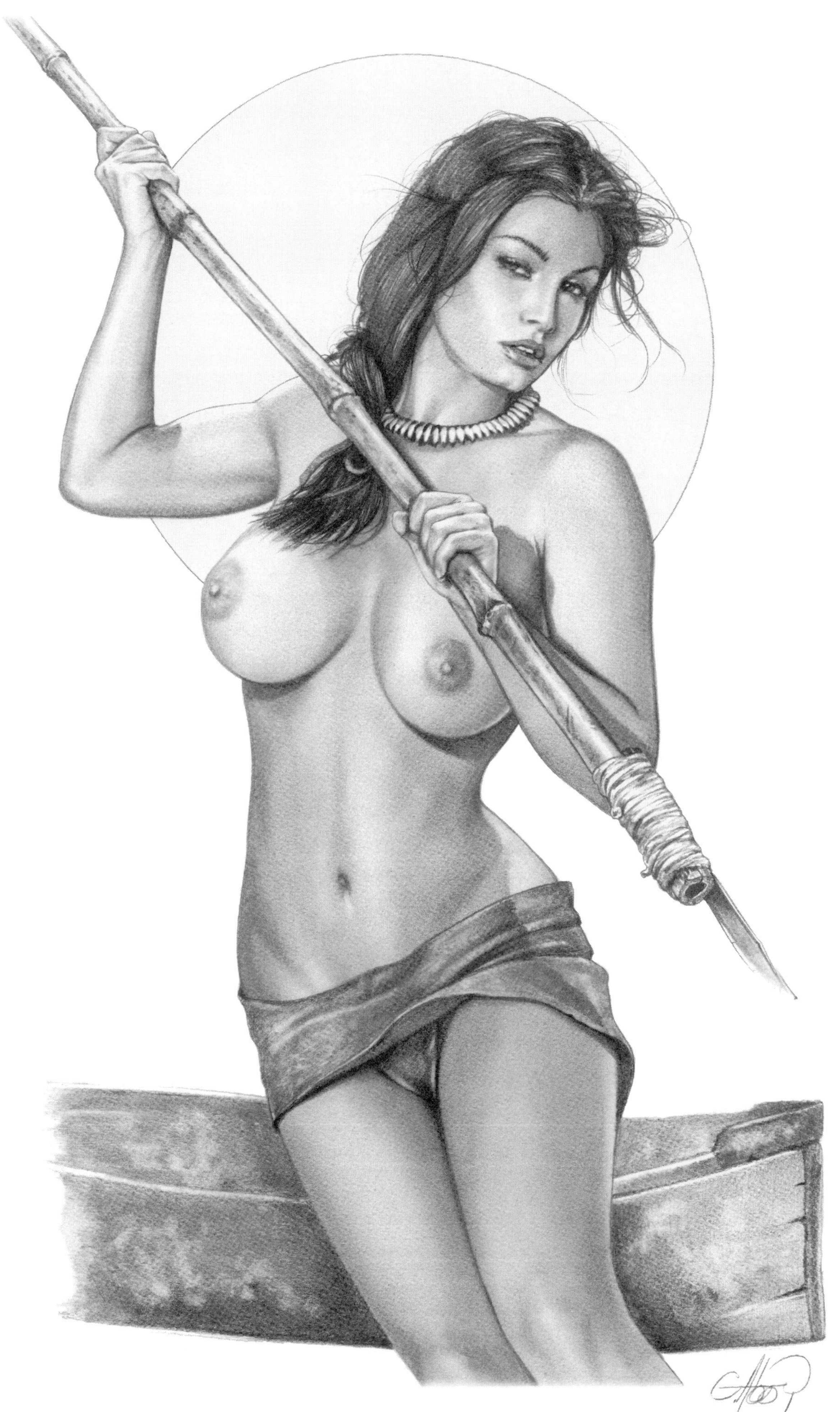

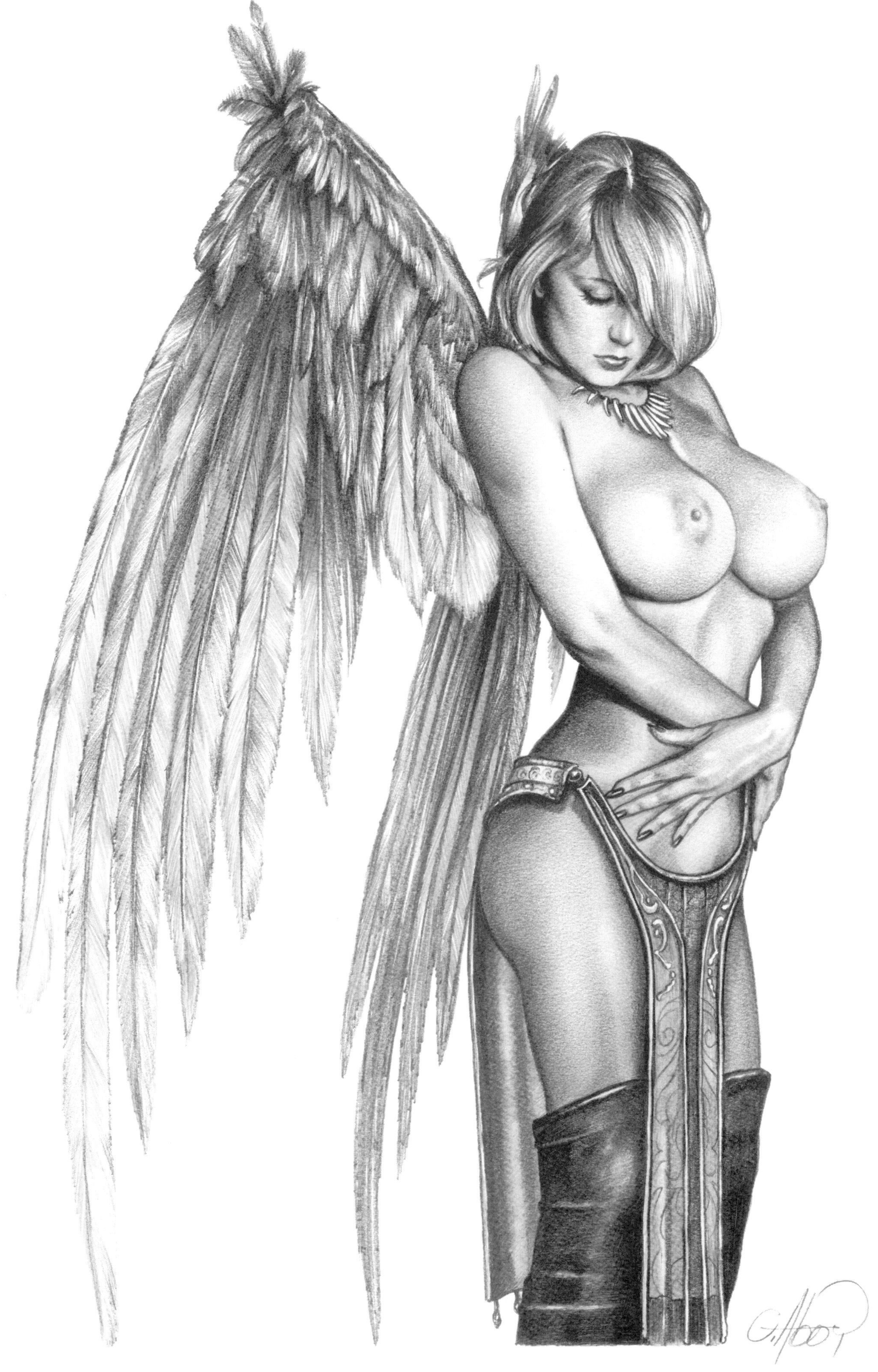

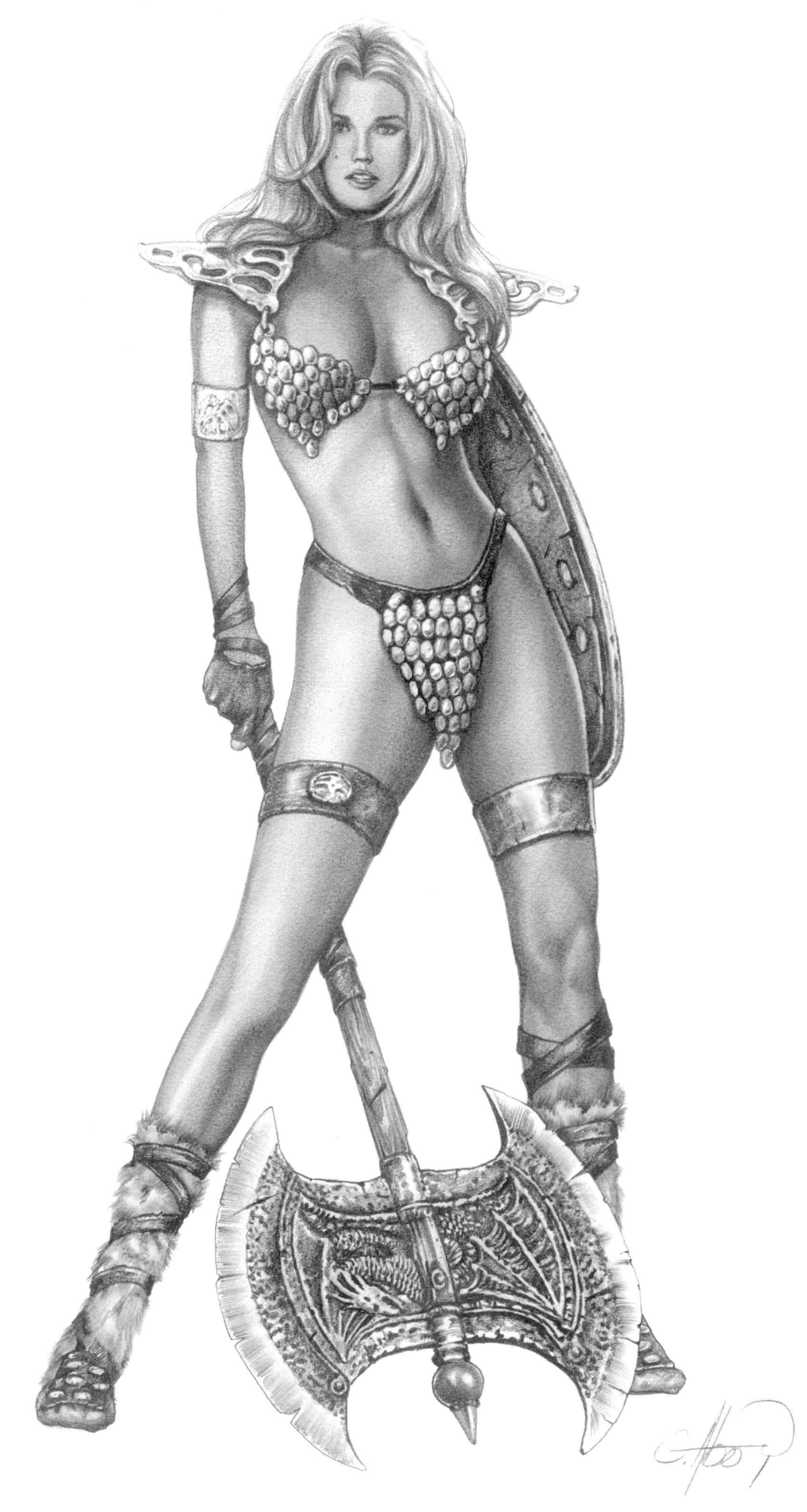

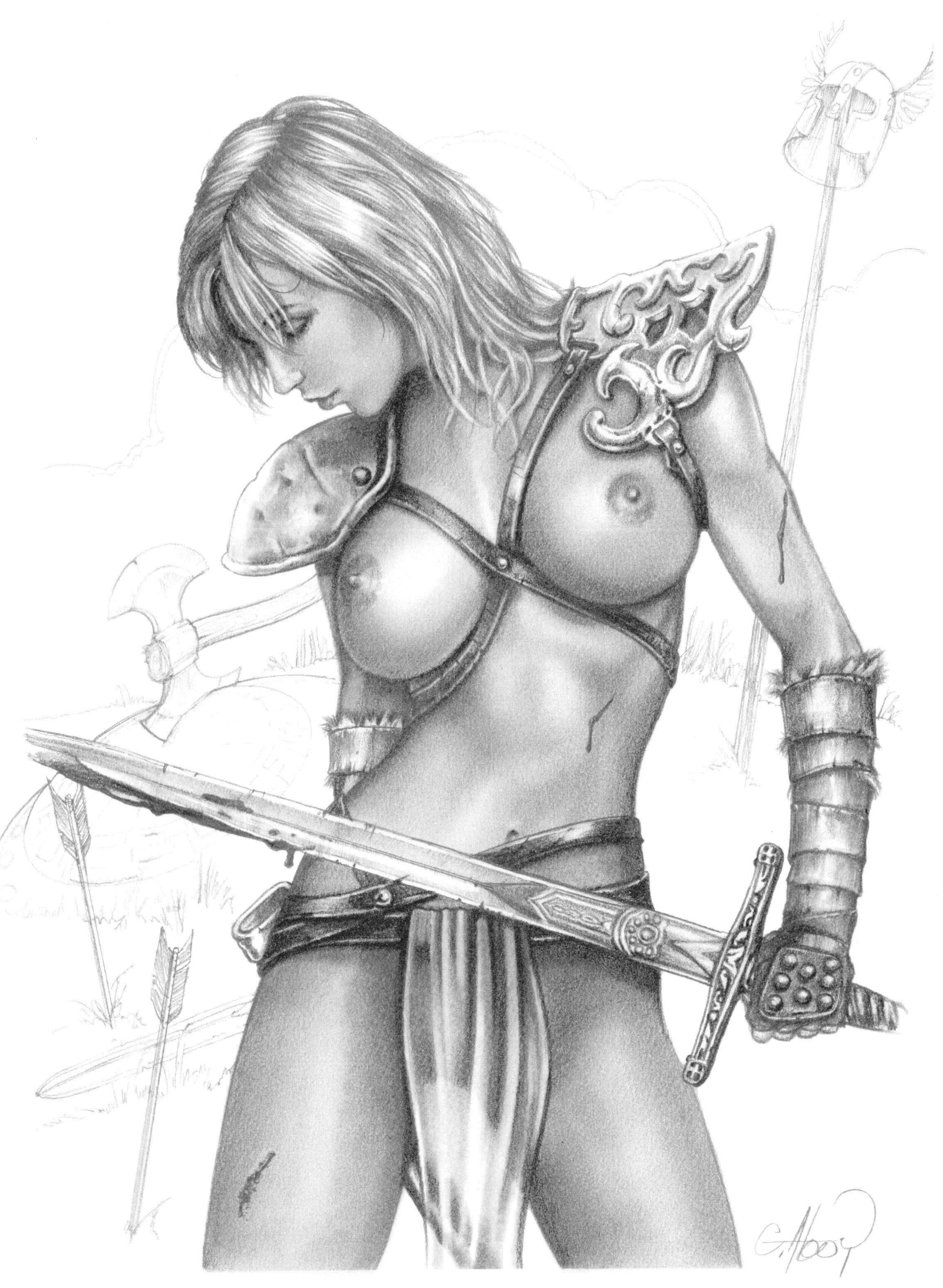

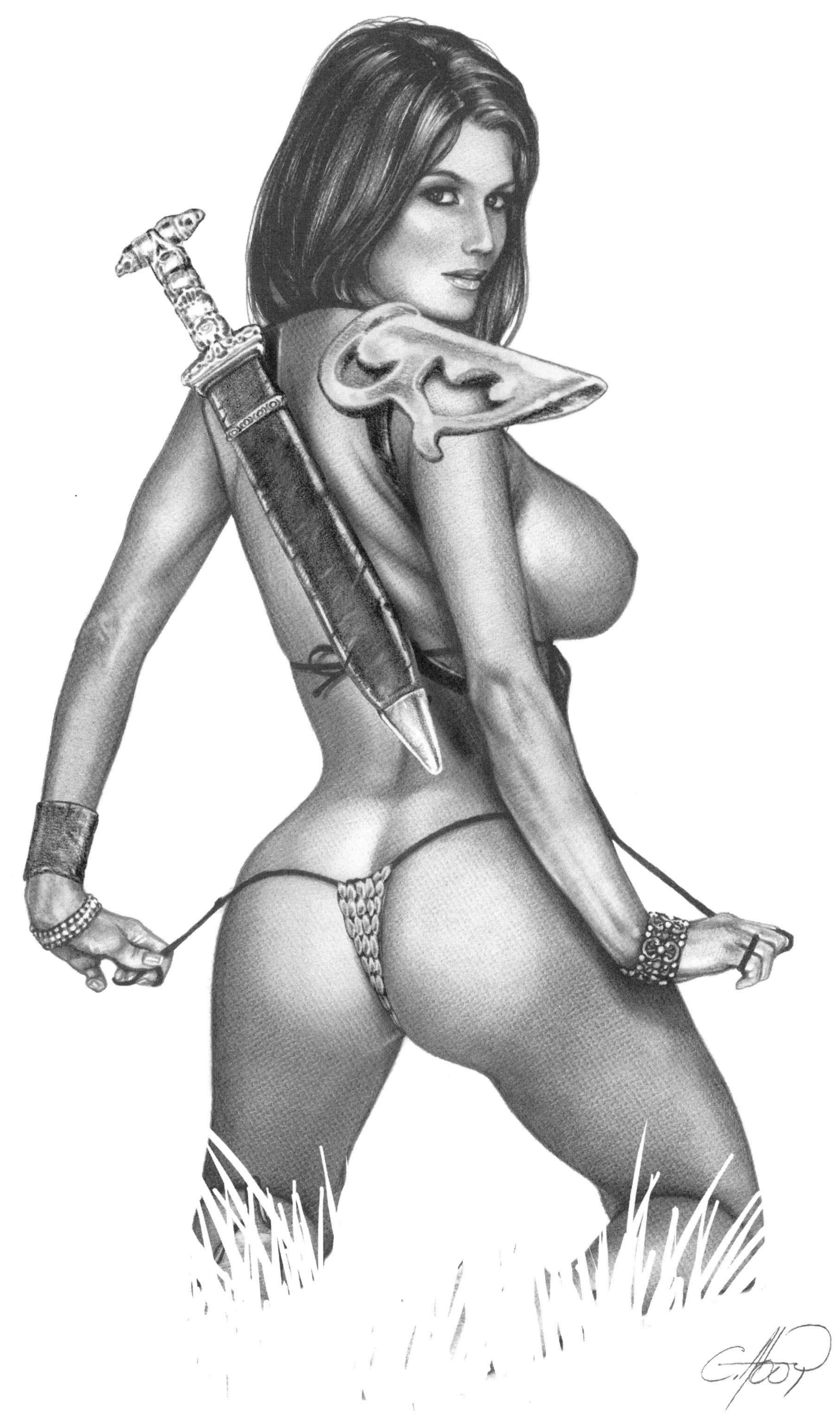

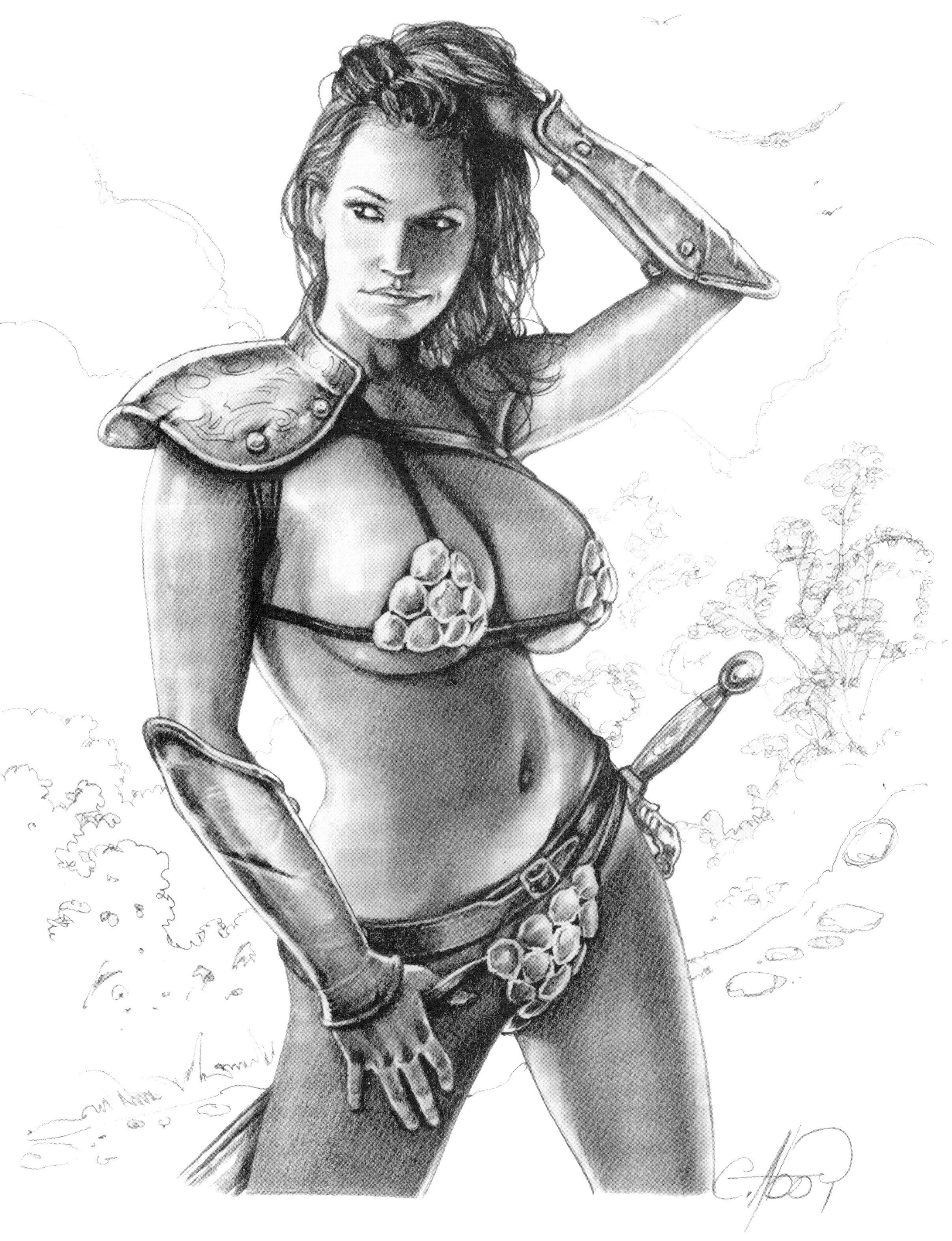

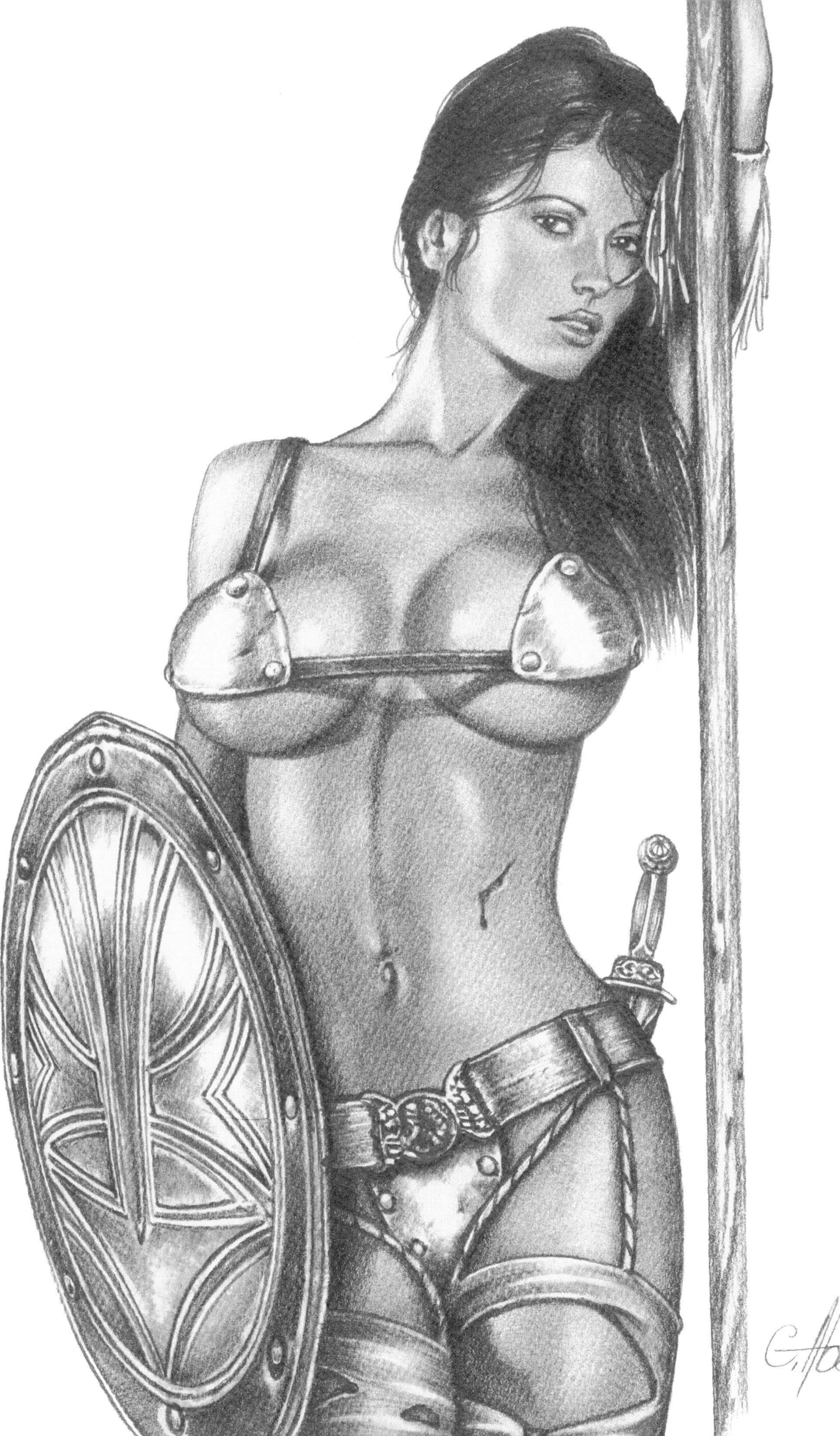

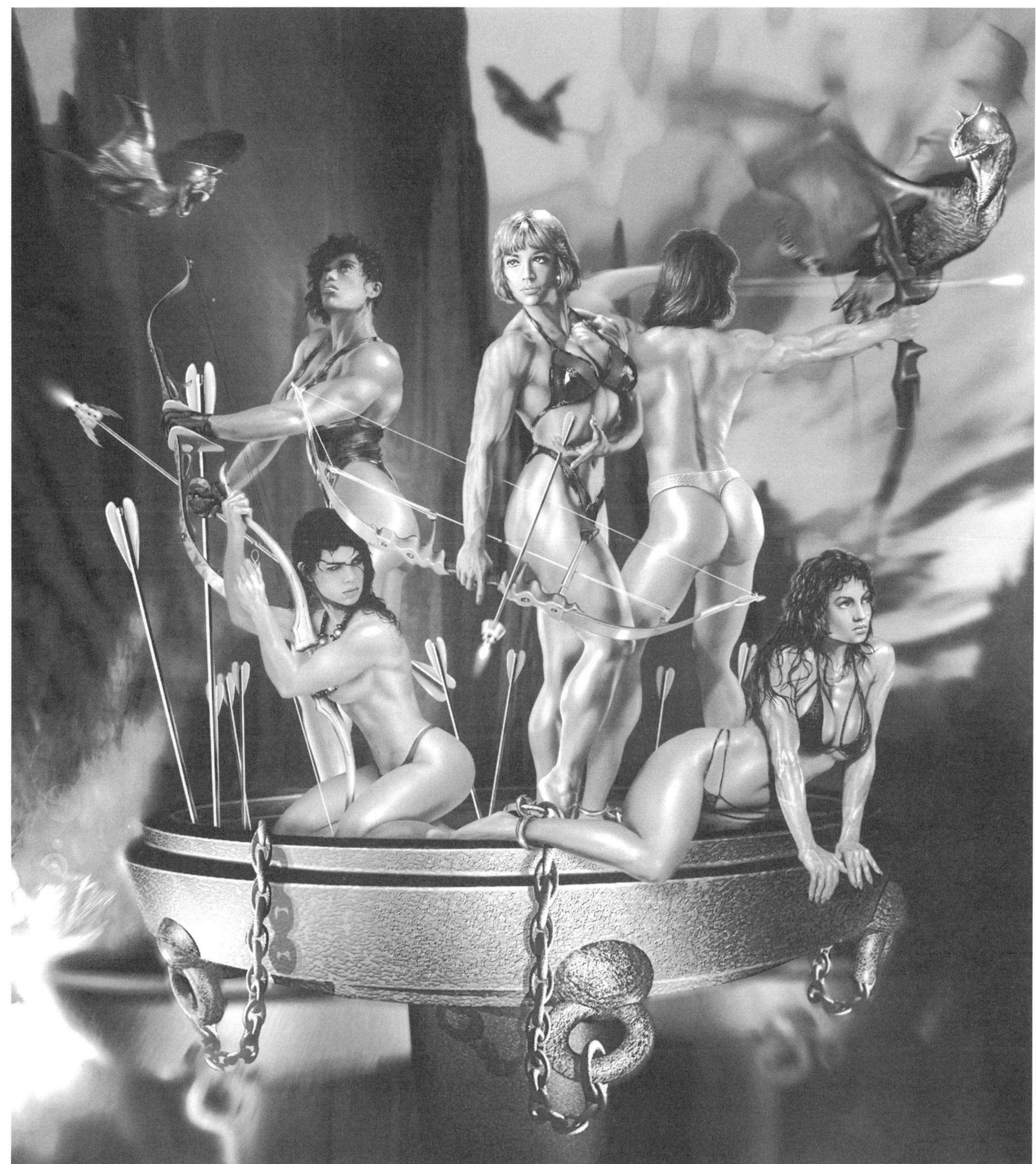

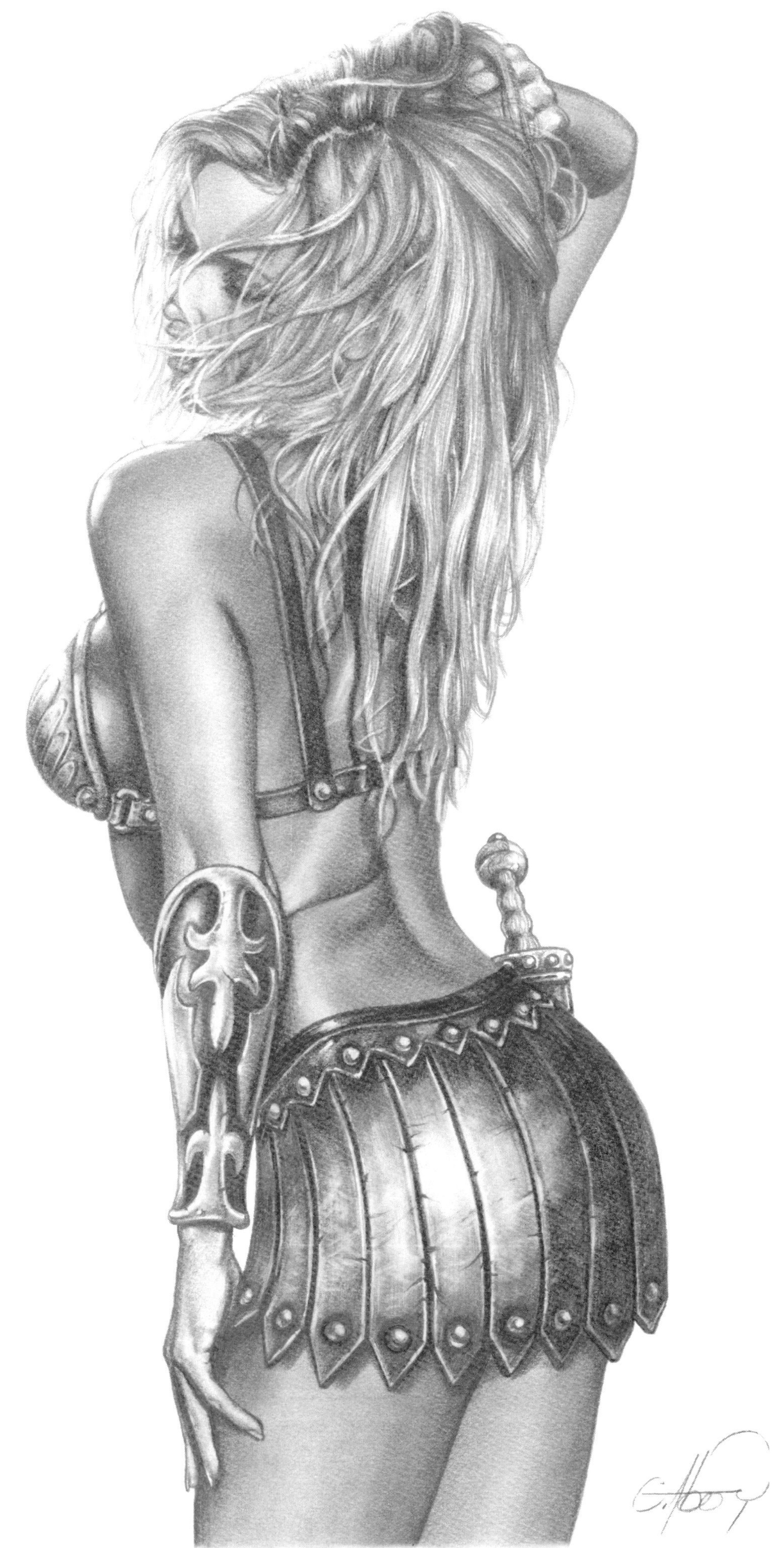

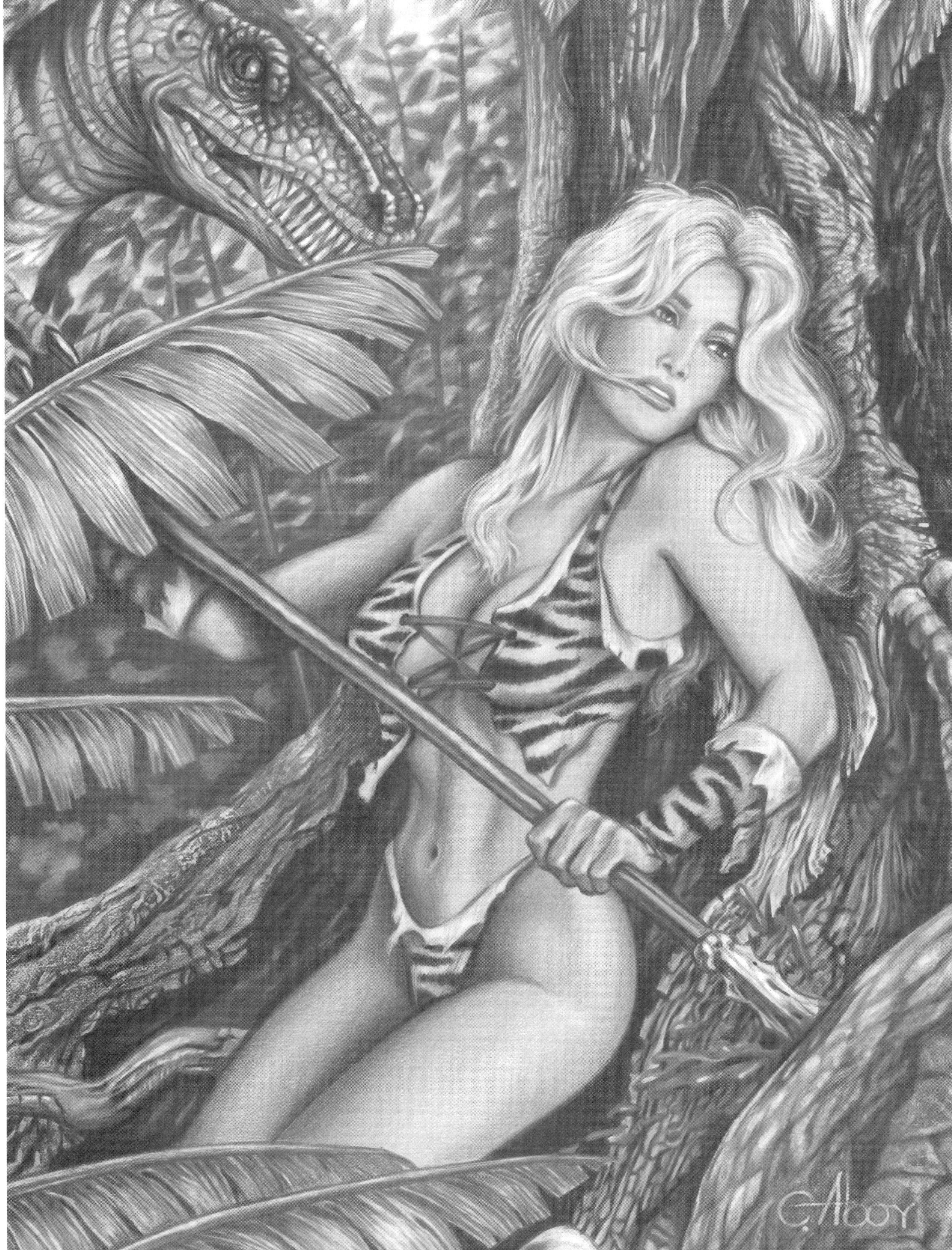
C. Aboy

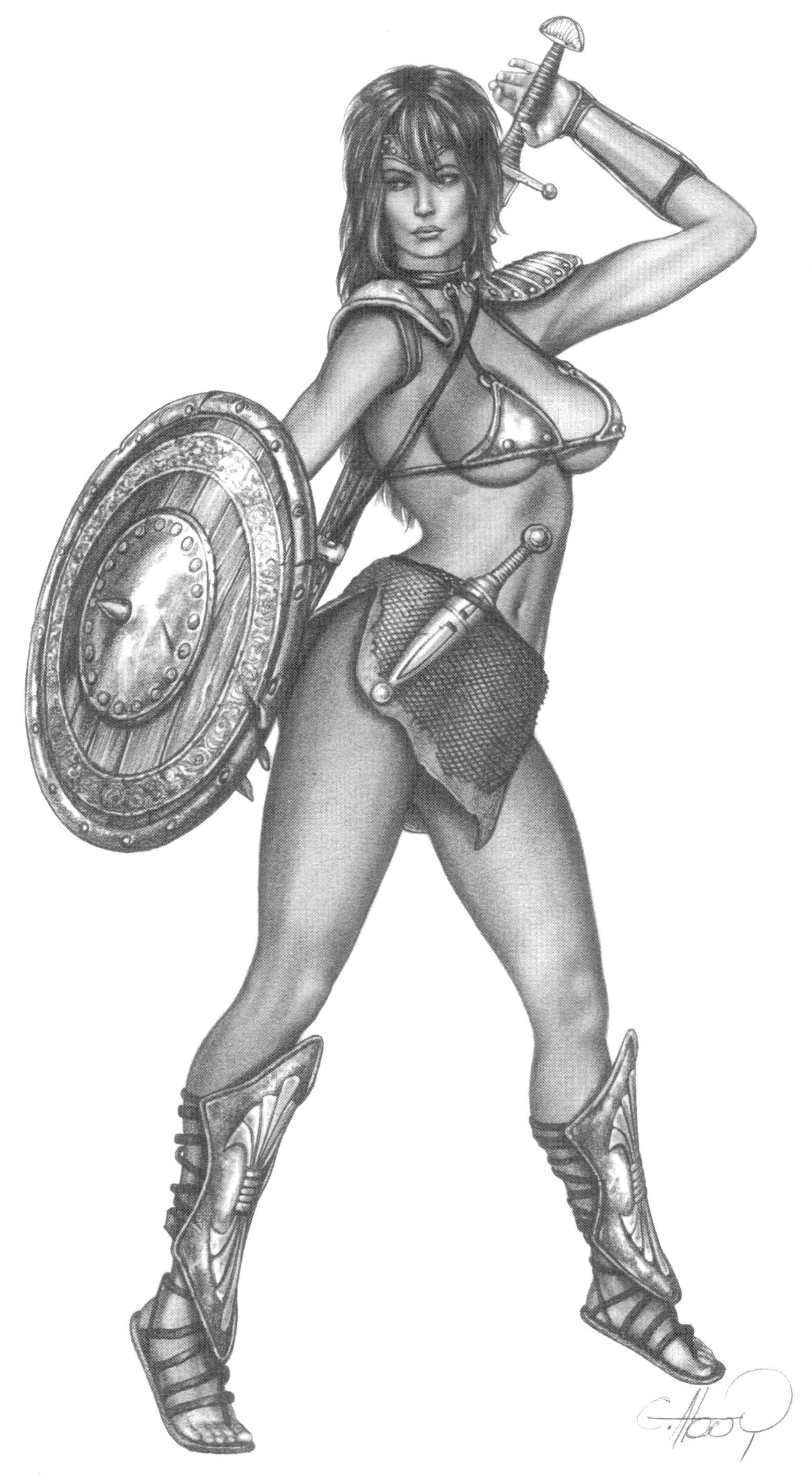

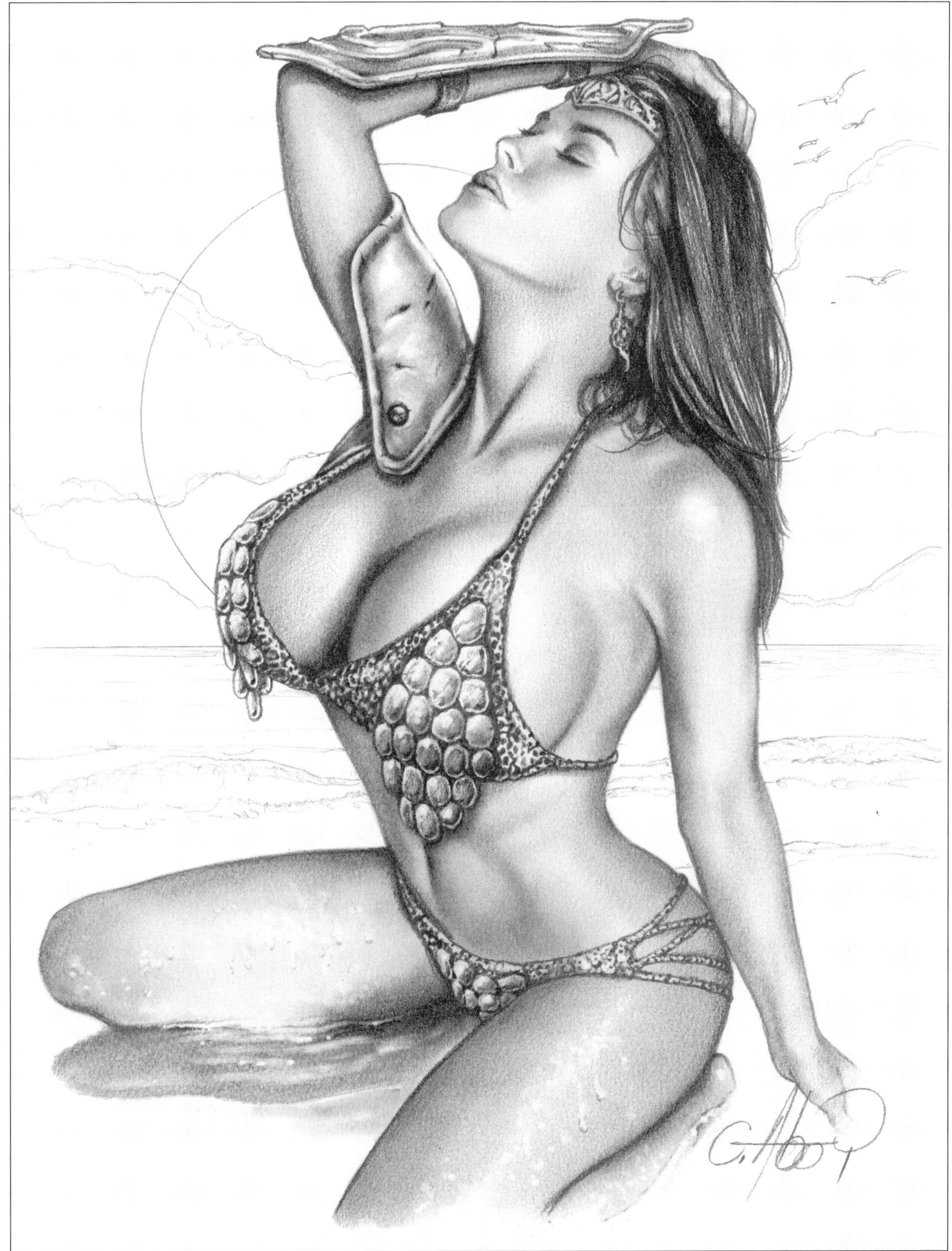

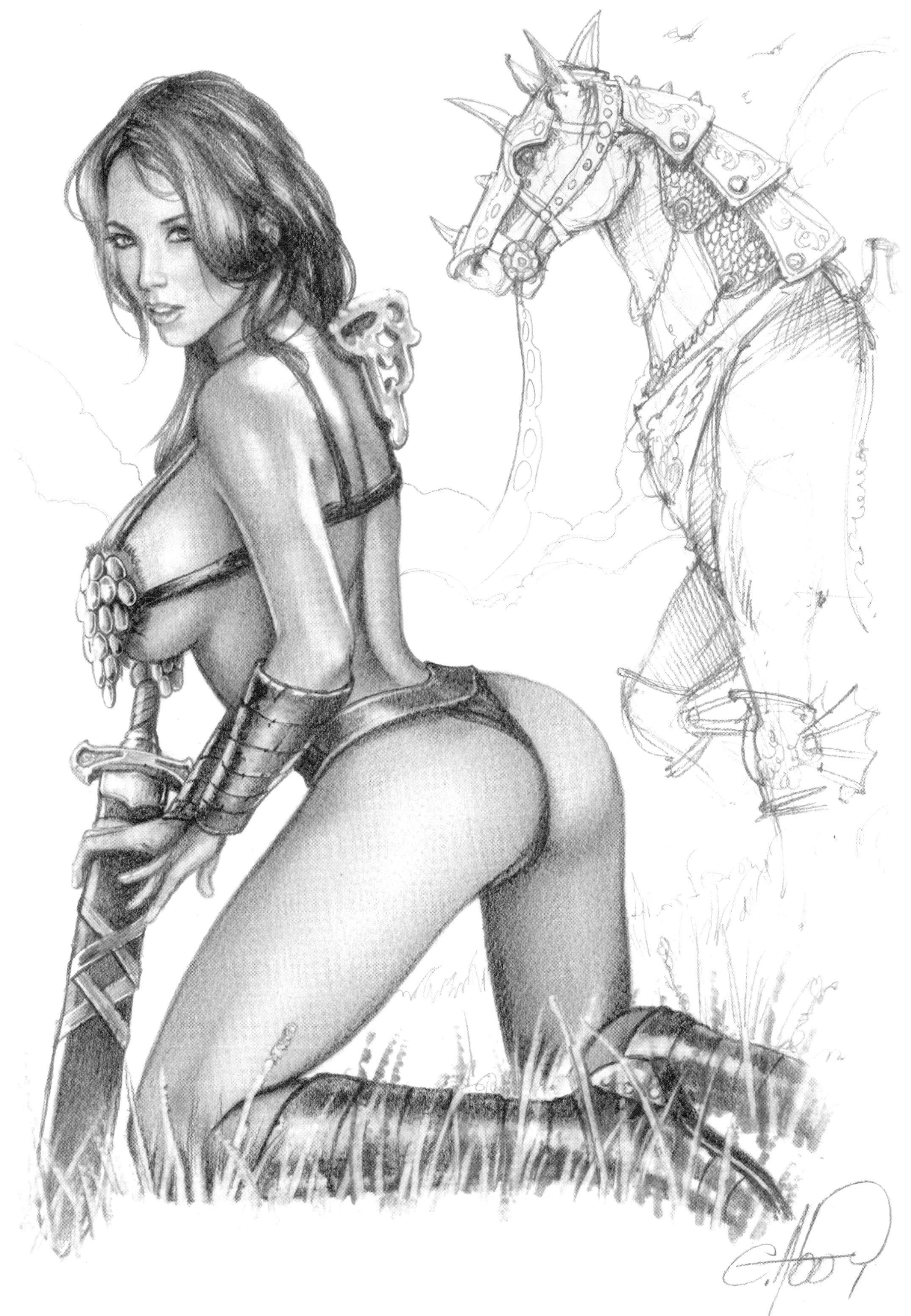

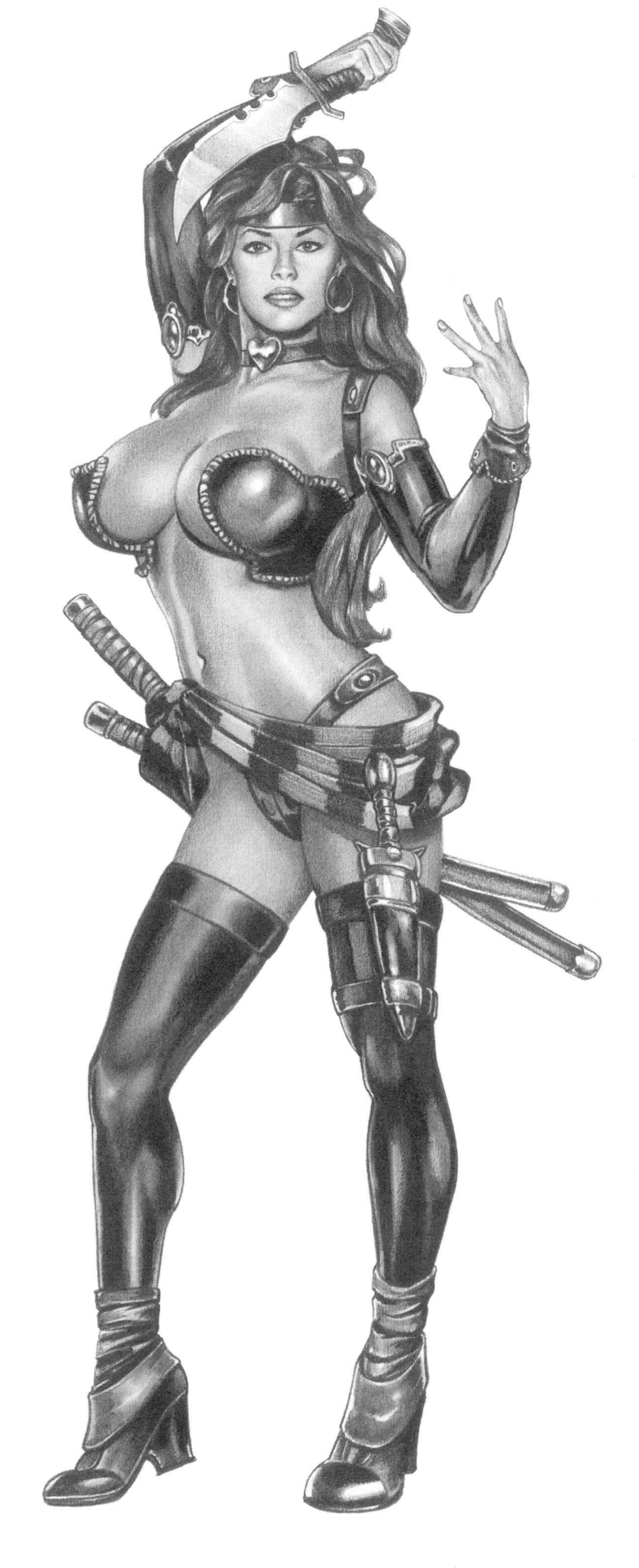

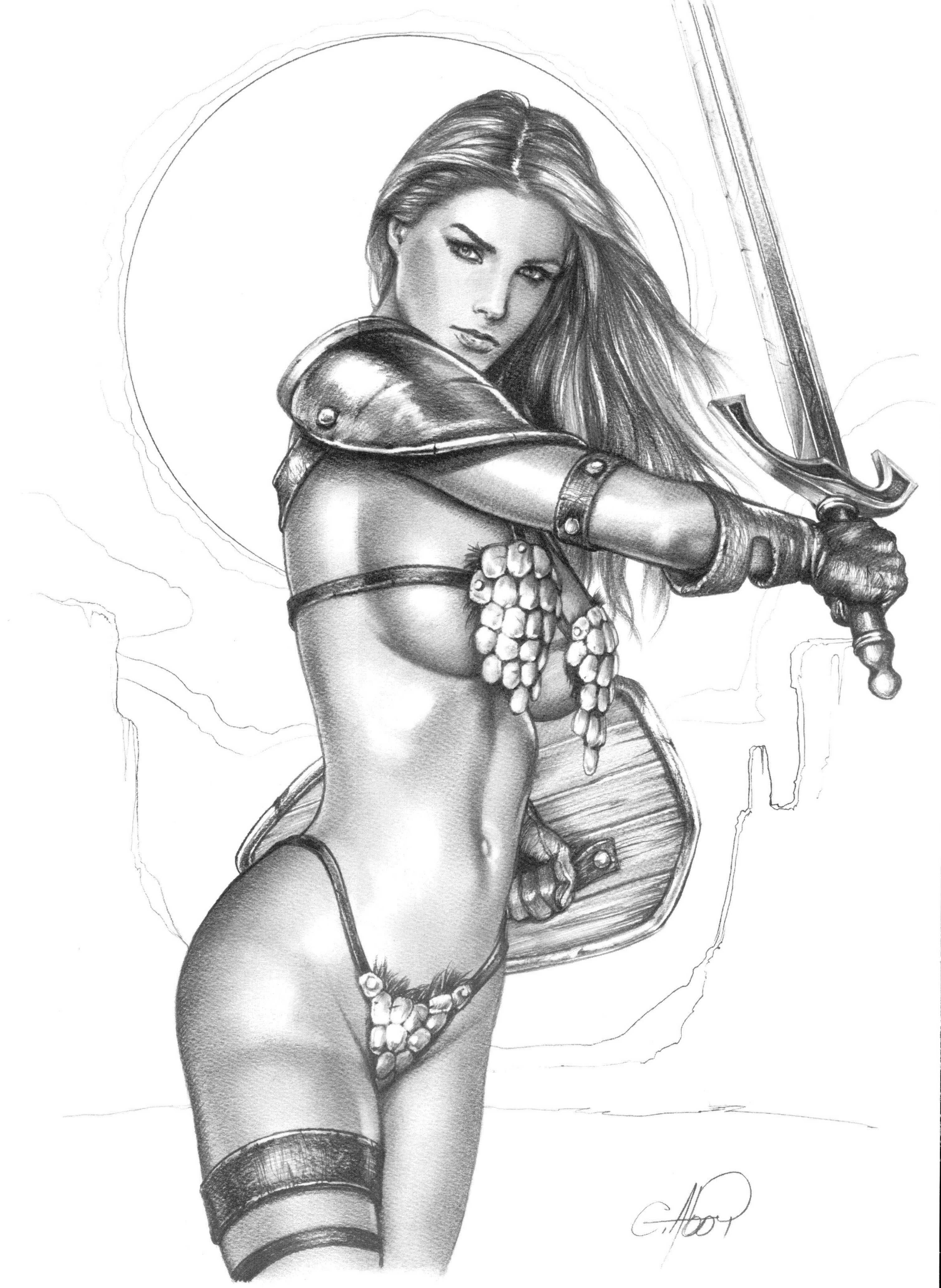

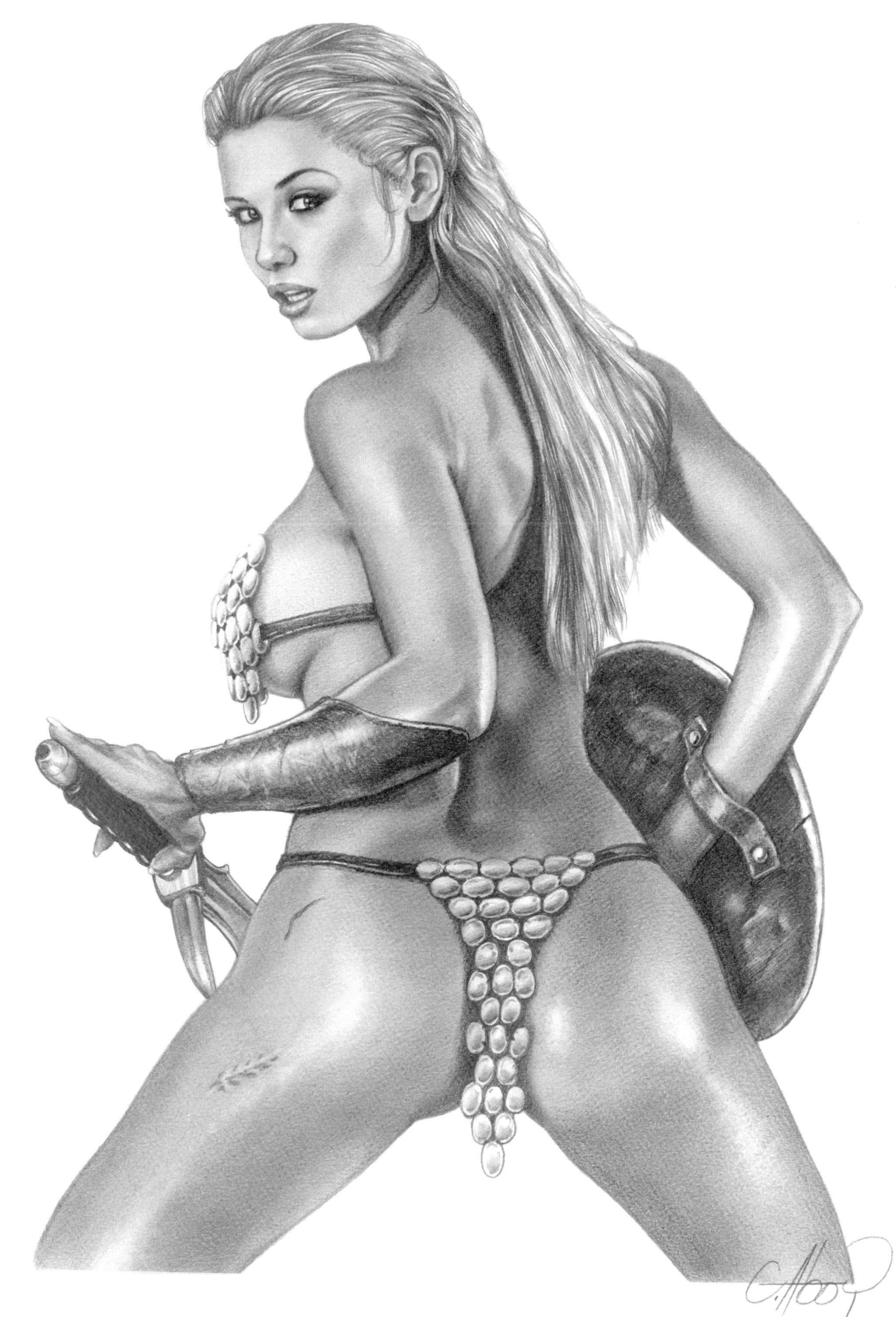

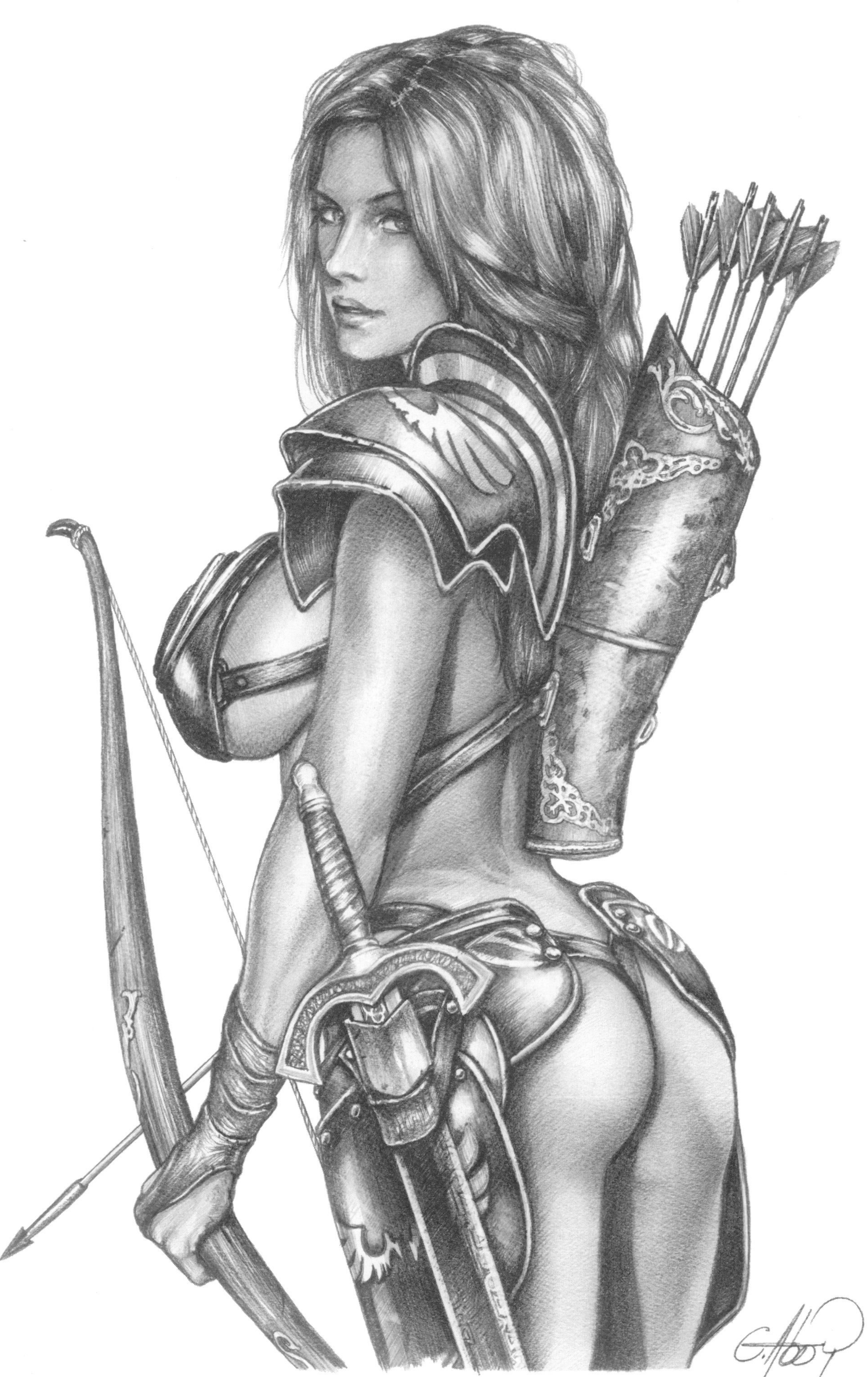